Seen in droplets sprayed on a piece of glass, a dancer leaps and leaps . . . and leaps. Each droplet acts as a lens. This kind of lens makes an upside down image. The photograph has been turned so the dancer appears right-side up. To make this picture, the photographer held the glass over a photograph of a dancer. Water acts as a mirror, too. Learn why on page 60.

BOOKS FOR WORLD EXPLORERS
NATIONAL GEOGRAPHIC SOCIETY

Contents

COVER: It's not a crystal ball, but it invites you to gaze within the pages of this book. Dazzling discoveries and surprises await you. Can you guess what's sparkling on the cover? Turn to page 103.
ROBERTO VILLA/LEO DE WYS INC.

LIKE LIVING LOOKOUT TOWERS, giraffes watch for danger on a dry African grassland. Their long necks help them see far into the distance. Their necks give these animals another advantage, too. Find out what it is on page 11.
© MARION PATTERSON/NAT'L AUDUBON SOC. COLL./PHOTO RESEARCHERS, INC.

Copyright © 1985 National Geographic Society
Library of Congress CIP data: p. 104

Since You Ask...

What questions spring to your mind when you look at this photograph? Does it make you want to ask, for example: *What is that odd-looking flying machine? What kind of airplane is that on the ground? Who is the man? What is he doing?*

Such questions have simple answers. The odd-looking aircraft is an airship named *White Dwarf*. The plane is a C-46 Commando. The man is a test pilot, Bryan Allen. Allen is trying out the airship while it is secured to the ground by lines called tethers.

Do the answers spark your curiosity? You may begin to think of harder questions—those that ask "how." *How does the* White Dwarf *stay aloft? How does it move from place to place?* The answers: Helium, a gas that is lighter than air, keeps the *White Dwarf* in the sky. Pedal power keeps it moving.

Questions that ask "why" may be the hardest of all. *Why did dinosaurs die out?* You'll find that question on page 84. When you read the answer, you will learn that scientists have various explanations for the disappearance of dinosaurs. They do not yet know which, if any, of the explanations is correct.

In *Why in the World?* you will find many different kinds of questions—asked by curious readers like you. *Do cats and dogs dream? What is a galaxy? How do babies learn to talk? Why is the sky blue?*

Why, you might ask, wouldn't every question in *Why in the World?* begin with the word "why"? The kinds of questions readers ask are as varied as the readers are themselves—that's why!

Body Works

Why do I get hiccups?

Hic! Suddenly, you hear yourself making a funny noise. *Hic!* There it is again. Here is what's happening. A dome-shaped muscle called the diaphragm (DIE-uh-fram) lies between your lungs and abdomen. Normally, it pulls air into your lungs at a relaxed pace. Now it moves in sudden jerks. With each jerk, air rushes into the lungs. The vocal cords react by snapping shut, blocking the airflow. The air hitting the vocal cords makes the sound. No one is sure what causes hiccups, though they often occur when you eat, laugh, or cry, or if you swallow air. Your friends may suggest "cures," like eating sugar, holding your breath, or asking someone to scare you. Luckily, hiccups usually go away in a short time.

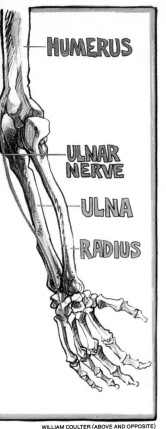

HUMERUS

ULNAR NERVE

ULNA

RADIUS

WILLIAM COULTER (ABOVE AND OPPOSITE)

Why does it hurt when I hit my funny bone?

Banging your funny bone isn't very humorous. But it does have to do with the humerus—the long bone in your upper arm. The humerus meets the radius and the ulna, bones in your lower arm, at your elbow. None of these bones, however, is your funny bone. There is no such bone. The tingly pain you feel when you bang your elbow comes from a nerve. The ulnar nerve, as you can see in the diagram, runs from your shoulder to your hand. When this nerve is pinched between your bones and a hard object, injury signals travel to the brain, and you feel pain. Unlike most nerves, which are protected by layers of muscle, the ulnar nerve crosses the elbow close to the surface of the skin. When the girl in the cartoon bumped her elbow, she jolted her ulnar nerve.

JAY LURIE/WEST STOCK

Why do babies have soft spots on their heads?

If this teenager were to look closely at the top of her three-day-old brother's head, she might see a pulse beating. The pulse is vibrating beneath a diamond-shaped patch of skin covering a soft spot. The plates of bone that form a baby's skull are soft and loosely connected at birth. The openings between the bones are called fontanels (fahnt-en-ELS), or soft spots.

Newborn babies normally have six fontanels. The one at the top of the skull toward the back is the largest. During birth, a baby must pass through a small opening in the mother's body. The skull squeezes together. The plates may overlap, covering the fontanels. Soon after birth, the head goes back to its natural shape. The soft spots are uncovered. In about three months, the skull begins to harden. New bone forms and fits together, filling in the openings. The process takes about two years. Meanwhile, anyone holding the baby has to be careful to protect its head.

Why does my skin wrinkle in the bath?

Some parts of the human body—especially the hands and feet—get a lot of wear and tear. All day, you use your hands. You walk and run on your feet. But these parts of your body come with equipment to help handle the pressure. A coating of protein covers your skin, protecting it and making it waterproof. The inside of your hands and the bottom of your feet have a thick layer of this coating, called keratin (KEHR-uht-en). The keratin on your fingertips and toes is extra loose. What happens when you soak in the bathtub for a long time? Your fingertips and toes get wrinkly—as this boy discovered. Water seeps into the thick keratin layer. It stretches out, somewhat like a sweater left soaking in the sink. The skin hangs in loose folds, causing the wrinkles.

WILLIAM COULTER (ALL)

Why do my ears pop in an airplane?

The eardrums—pieces of skin stretched across the entrance to the middle ear—are supersensitive to changes in air pressure. Normally, the pressure inside your ears is the same as the pressure in the air around you. During an airplane takeoff, the pressure outside your ears becomes less than the pressure inside. Your eardrums bulge outward, then return to normal with a pop. You feel discomfort until passages called eustachian (you-STAY-she-uhn) tubes open. They allow air inside your middle ears to rush out. You can make this happen more quickly by yawning, swallowing, or chewing gum. Once you are in the air, the pressure inside and outside your ears remains equal—until you begin to descend. Then *pop* go the ears again.

What makes a person snore?

Zzzzzz. A buzzing sound echoes through a bedroom. It doesn't come from a saw. It comes from a person who is sleeping peacefully—and making a racket snoring.

Scientists think that more than 30 million Americans snore. Some snore almost every night. Others snore now and then. Most snorers make the noise when they sleep on their backs—like the boy below.

Maybe you have used a blade of grass to make a whistle. When you held the grass and blew air past it, the blade vibrated and created a sound. Snoring works in a similar way. As the boy lies in bed, gravity pulls his tongue backward. Gravity also pulls on various soft tissues, including a dangly piece of flesh at the top of his throat called the uvula (YOU-vyuh-luh). The tissues partially block the airway leading to his lungs. As the boy inhales, air rushes through the narrow opening and causes the soft parts of his mouth to vibrate. That makes the whistling, snorting, buzzing noises we call snoring.

Animal Oddities

CLIFF HOLLENBECK PHOTO

Why are dolphins so easily trained?

If you have visited a marine park, you probably know which animals steal the show: the dolphins. They delight visitors with their stunts. They ring bells, blow horns, and play basketball. Using their powerful tail fins, they "walk" backward in the water, as the bottlenose dolphin at left is doing.

Social, playful, and curious, dolphins get along well with humans. They learn to do tricks quickly. Sometimes they make up their own. To teach a dolphin to do tricks, a trainer uses its natural abilities. For example, dolphins often jump out of the water. So it's a short step to teaching the animals to jump through hoops or over bars. Underwater, dolphins use a sonar system of rapid clicks to navigate. With this system, a dolphin can pinpoint an object tossed into the water by a trainer. The animal can retrieve the object within seconds.

Dolphins, also called porpoises, are toothed whales. They are not fish, but mammals—animals that, as babies, drink milk from their mothers. Mammals include such intelligent animals as monkeys and apes. Yet some scientists think that dolphins, with their large, well-developed brains, may possess more intelligence than do monkeys and apes.

To communicate with one another, dolphins whistle, squeak, growl, or moan. Some scientists think that these animals eventually can be trained to communicate with humans through a language of signs and symbols.

Why do giraffes have such long necks?

On the dry grasslands of Africa, a giraffe's long neck gives the animal a big lift (right). A giraffe reaches high into the trees to find a plentiful supply of leaves and twigs. It simply lifts its head and stretches out its long, flexible tongue.

No other plant-eating animal of the grasslands can reach as high as the giraffe, the tallest animal on earth. Other animals feed lower down. The giraffe's height allows it to nibble the leaves of its favorite tree, the acacia, without competition.

Its long neck gives the giraffe another advantage as well: a good view. An adult giraffe can see for long distances. It can easily spot a lion—its main enemy—in time to get away.

Does the neck have any drawbacks? One big one. For a thirsty giraffe, it's a long way down to take a drink. To reach the water, a giraffe has to spread its front legs wide apart. In this awkward position, the animal becomes an easy target for enemies.

DAVID CAYLESS/OXFORD SCIENTIFIC FILMS

Why don't spiders get caught in their own webs?

Many spiders trap prey on sticky threads in their webs. The spiders themselves avoid the threads as they weave. The orb weaver (above) uses dry silk for the spokes that form the framework. Next, working outward from the center in a circular pattern, it lays down more dry threads. Using those threads for footing, it reverses direction. It replaces the dry threads with sticky ones. If a leg becomes caught on a sticky thread, the spider moistens the leg with saliva. A chemical in the saliva dissolves the silk.

Why do flies rub their legs together?

Chances are, the fly that lands on your picnic table isn't resting. It's probably busy rubbing its legs together. Bristly hairs cover a fly's body and legs. The hairs trap dirt. When the fly rubs its legs together, it is cleaning itself by scraping those hairs.

How can birds sit on power lines without being electrocuted?

Outdoor power lines can be dangerous. Some carry huge amounts of electricity. Yet birds often perch on power lines without getting hurt (above). The birds aren't touching any object through which electricity can flow to the ground. For electricity to travel from a line to the ground or from line to line, it needs a conductor—something through which it can flow. If a bird perches on a line and touches a nearby tree or utility pole, it may be electrocuted. The bird and the tree or pole would be conductors of electricity from the line to the ground. Also, if a bird touches two lines at once, it may be electrocuted. Electricity would travel from line to line through the bird.

How do male bighorn sheep fight each other?

Every fall, at the start of the mating season, male bighorn sheep have noisy and spectacular head-butting contests. The animals that win the most battles may become leaders of the herd. The winning males usually have first choice of the females.

When fighting, the males, called rams, rear up on their hind legs. They tilt their heads to the side, showing off their huge, curved horns. *Crack!* The rams collide head-on (right). The sound of the crash can be heard as far as a mile away. The animals may fight repeatedly, sometimes for hours. Their double-layered skulls help protect them from serious injury. The battle ends when one ram gives up.

Why do roosters crow in the morning?

Actually, roosters do not crow *only* in the morning. They crow throughout the day. A sudden change in temperature or a loud noise at any time may make a rooster crow. If an intruder enters a rooster's territory, the animal may crow. However, people are more likely to notice the rooster's crowing in the quiet of morning. It may be the first loud noise they hear, so it wakes them up.

Whatever the time of day, a rooster's cock-a-doodle-doo may mean several things. With head held high and tail erect, a rooster loudly crows to other roosters and hens. He announces, "Here I am," or "This is my territory."

Most of the crowing in a barnyard is done by roosters. However, in rare instances, hens too have been known to crow.

Clean and Dirty

Why do pigs lie in the mud?

Taking a snooze in a mudhole may not sound very appealing to you. To a pig, however, a mud bath means coolness, comfort, and protection from bothersome insects. After all, a pig can't buy insect repellent or sunscreen the way you can.

A thick coating of mud protects the pig's sensitive skin from bites and from the sun's burning rays. The

Why do lions and other cats have rough tongues?

This lion can be fierce—but underneath that bushy mane and tan coat is an animal similar in many ways to a pet cat. Has a cat ever licked you? If so, you know that its tongue feels like coarse sandpaper. That's because tough bits of flesh, called papillae (puh-PIL-ee), stick up from the center of its tongue. The papillae work much like the bristles of a hairbrush. When a cat brushes its coat with its tongue, the papillae remove dust, dirt, and loose hair. All cats use their tongues for grooming.

A cat can clean almost all of its body with its tongue, but it can't reach its head and neck. To clean those areas, the cat first licks a paw. Then it rubs the damp paw over its fur, as if it were using a washcloth. You've probably seen house cats wash their heads and necks in this way. At a zoo, you can see big cats using the same method. A cat's tongue has another job, too. The papillae are tough enough to scrape meat from a bone. A cat's tongue is quite a gadget—a brush and a knife and fork combined in one rough package.

mud also helps keep the animal cool. With very few sweat glands, pigs cannot cool off by sweating. On hot days, they may pant as dogs do. But stretching out in cool mud is an even better way of escaping the heat of a summer afternoon. That's what the contented creature below is doing.

Some people think that pigs are dirty animals because of their habit of bathing in mud. Actually, pigs are very clean animals. Their relatives, wild hogs, seek out clean, fresh water for cooling off. And when barnyard pigs are given a choice, they prefer bathing in cool water to lying in the mud. Many farmers help their pigs beat the heat by giving them frequent showers.

Pet Puzzlers

Do cats and dogs dream?

If three little kittens really did lose their mittens, they might have dreamed about it the same night. Cats and dogs do dream. In their dreams, they probably relive exciting or frightening events of the day.

When scientists studied the sleep of cats in a laboratory, they found that the cats first went into a quiet state of sleep. The cats' eyes moved slowly under the lids. Then, after a few minutes, the eyes moved rapidly and jerkily. Brain-wave recordings showed that the animals had entered a sleep state called REM—for rapid eye movement. Throughout their sleep, the animals passed back and forth between the deeper quiet state and REM sleep.

Humans experience the same sleep states. Studies have shown that humans dream only during REM sleep, so scientists think that cats and dogs dream then as well. Scientists believe that REM sleep serves a useful purpose for cats and dogs. In this state, the animals sleep lightly. They wake from time to time and inspect their surroundings for danger.

A dog that is dreaming may whine, pant, bark, and wag its tail. Sometimes, it makes running movements. A cat usually lies more quietly, but it may twitch, or swat with its paw.

If your sleeping pet appears restless, don't worry. It's probably just living in a dream world.

WILLIAM COULTER

Why do dogs pant?

The Siberian husky at left is panting to cool off. All dogs stick out their tongues and pant when they are overheated. Unlike people, dogs do not cool off by perspiring. When you perspire, drops of sweat evaporate from your skin. As the moisture escapes into the air, it cools you. As the dog pants, its breath blows away moisture from its mouth, nose, and lungs. The escaping moisture cools the dog.

Why are dogs able to swim without being taught?

Dogs are born with a natural ability to swim. A month-old puppy that has never been in water will move its legs in a swimming motion if you hold it over a tub of water. By the time it is two months old, a large pup may swim well. Dogs and other four-legged animals have two advantages. When they enter the water, they are already in a floating position. And because their weight is evenly distributed, they float easily. Dogs of some breeds—such as the Labrador retriever above—can swim long distances. Some dogs, however, are water shy. It can take a lot of coaxing to get a reluctant dog to dog-paddle.

How and why do cats purr?

According to an old folktale, a dying prince would be saved only if the princess who loved him could spin 10,000 spools of thread in a few weeks. The princess couldn't do the job alone. Her three cats helped her, working hard at three tiny spinning wheels. For their efforts, the cats were rewarded with the ability to purr—to make a noise like the whir of a spinning wheel.

People have long admired the cat's purr. But until recently, scientists were not exactly sure how cats made this sound. Now scientists know that the cat has the ability to narrow the space in its larynx (LAR-inx), or voice box. Air passes through the larynx on the way to and from the lungs. By narrowing the space, the cat disturbs the smooth flow of air. You hear the resulting rough flow of air as a purr. By listening carefully, you can hear slightly different tones when the cat inhales and when it exhales.

Mother cats often purr as they feed their kittens. The kittens purr when they are nursing. Adult cats purr a greeting to other cats and to people. In general, a purr is similar to a human smile. At times, however, the meaning is more difficult to explain—a cat may purr when it is near death after an illness.

Big cats, such as lions and tigers, purr just as house cats do. Fortunately for pet owners, house cats cannot roar like lions and tigers.

How do parrots talk?

If you want to keep a secret, don't tell it to a parrot. The bird might repeat it.

Parrots can copy the sounds of human speech in any language. The bird's vocal organ, called a syrinx (SIHR-inx), produces the sounds. Muscles in the syrinx tighten and relax by turns, helping the bird make noise.

In the wild, parrots imitate only the sounds of other parrots. Pet parrots, however, copy a variety of sounds. They imitate barking dogs and creaking doors. They whistle and sing.

Parrots are able to connect certain sounds with other sounds. That is why, for example, a parrot can be trained to respond to the ring of a telephone and a human voice saying "hello." The parrot will make a connection between the ringing of the telephone and the word. Soon it may squawk "hello" when the telephone rings.

Parrots are the most famous talkers of the bird world. But other birds, such as the black-billed magpie, the myna, and the crow, also can imitate human language.

WILLIAM COULTER (ALL)

Why can dogs hear sounds that people can't?

As this boy blows a whistle, his dog perks its ears and comes running. The boy has a Galton whistle, or silent whistle. The dog hears it, but the boy doesn't.

"Silent" sounds—those you can't hear—are all around you all the time. Dogs can hear more of these sounds than you can. Your dog can pick up sounds that are too high for your ears to detect. It can also hear fainter sounds than you can.

Every time an object moves and disturbs something, such as air, vibrations begin in the disturbed substance. These vibrations are called sound waves. Sound waves travel at different rates. The more vibrations per second, the higher the pitch of the sound. A bird's song, for example, sets up faster vibrations than a bass fiddle does.

The ear is a sound receiver. When vibrating waves strike your ear—or your dog's—small bones begin to vibrate. One bone starts fluid vibrating in a part of the ear called the cochlea (KOH-klee-uh). There, cells change the vibrations to nerve impulses that travel to the brain. The human ear can pick up sound waves that vibrate between 20 and 20,000 times a second. A dog's ear has a more sensitive cochlea. It can detect as many as 50,000 vibrations a second.

In addition to hearing higher and fainter sounds than you do, your dog can tell the difference between very similar sounds. If you have trained your dog to come at the sound of a silent whistle—or one you can hear—don't change it. Your sharp-eared pet might pay no attention to a new sound.

Out to Lunch

How can a snake swallow something larger than its head?

Can you open your mouth wide enough to swallow a beach ball? Of course not! But if you could, that astonishing feat would be similar to what many snakes do with ease.

Snakes that eat large meals whole must be able to open their mouths extra wide. The structure of their lower jaws helps them do this. The lower jaw is divided into left and right halves. At the front, the halves are joined by flexible connective tissue that allows them to spread wide apart. Leverlike bones at the skull permit the halves to swing far downward. At right, you can see how wide the African egg-eating snake opens its mouth to surround a chicken egg.

Gulp! As the snake swallows, part of its body looks swollen (below). The skin of its head and neck expands greatly. Neck muscles will squeeze the egg against sharp spines on the underside of the snake's backbone. When the shell breaks, the liquid part of the egg will move to the snake's stomach. The snake will bring up most of the broken shell and spit it out.

JOHN VISSER/BRUCE COLEMAN INC.

JOHN VISSER/BRUCE COLEMAN LTD.

STEPHEN J. KRASEMANN/DRK PHOTO

Why do ducks duck their heads under the water?

When you're feeling hungry, you probably head for the kitchen. When certain kinds of ducks decide it's time for a snack, they often go bottoms up, like the two mallards above. If you could look under the water, you'd see the ducks stretching their necks out, looking for food. With their bills, they find seeds and other duck delicacies on the muddy bottom.

Mallards are the most plentiful kind of waterfowl in North America. They are known as dabblers—ducks that tip themselves over in shallow water to feed. Dabblers live in ponds, lakes, rivers, and marshes in North America, Europe, and Asia.

The next time you spot a duck, wait around to see if it suddenly goes bill down, tail up. If it does, you'll know you're watching a dabbler that is seeking a snack.

Why do moths make holes in sweaters?

To you, a wool sweater is something to wear. To this insect, it's a meal. Actually, the adult clothes moth is not the destructive creature that chomps holes in your wool sweaters. But adult females do lay eggs that hatch into *very* hungry caterpillars. The caterpillars, called larvae, eat wool sweaters—or fur coats, or silk dresses, or wool carpets.

A female clothes moth lays large numbers of eggs on clothing or carpets. When the eggs hatch, tiny larvae appear. They immediately start munching. Clothes moth larvae eat mainly substances that originally came from animals. They feast on wool from sheep, silk from silkworms, and fur from minks, foxes, and other animals. In a pinch, they will eat almost any dead animal matter or dead plant matter. But they don't normally eat artificial fibers, like polyester, or plant fibers, like cotton.

WILLIAM COULTER

Perfect Timing

TERRY DOMICO/EARTH IMAGES (ALL, THIS PAGE)

How do migrating salmon find their way back to the place where they hatched?

1) Flame-colored sockeye salmon return from the ocean to the freshwater stream where they hatched. There, they will deposit their eggs in gravel nests. Like all Pacific salmon, the sockeyes will die after their eggs are laid. **2)** A new generation of salmon begins life as pea-size eggs. You can see the eyes of the developing young within. **3)** After hatching, young salmon live for a time in fresh water. As they grow, their bodies change to suit salt water. Then, from thousands of freshwater streams and rivers, they migrate out to sea. Salmon spend one or more years in salt water. They may travel far from their hatching places. But when ready to reproduce, they return to the same stream in which they hatched.

Salmon migration is a very complicated process. Scientists think that the position of the sun and the stars, and differences in the earth's magnetic fields may help guide the fish from the oceans. The differences in the water's temperature and chemical makeup may also help the fish find their way inland. At the coast, where rivers and streams empty into the ocean, the salmons' sense of smell takes over. The fish remember the odor of their native streams. Battling the currents, the adults follow this odor to the spot where they began life.

BILL ROSS/WEST LIGHT

How can flowers bloom in the snow?

On the slopes of Mount Rainier, in Washington State, large packs of snow and ice cover the ground for most of the year. Yet two glacier lilies have poked through the snow (above). Before the lily bulbs could start to grow underground, they had to go through a chilling period. Then, as the weather grew warmer, increasing temperatures caused the bulbs to sprout. In places where the sun's rays penetrated the snow and warmed the soil, the lilies burst forth. The young plants had bullet-shaped leaves that helped them push through to the surface. You can see glacier lilies on snowy mountainsides in parts of the United States and Canada. Other mountain wildflowers, such as buttercups and avalanche lilies, have also adapted to frosty homes.

How do birds know when to migrate?

Flying on a straight course, sandhill cranes head north to their summer home. Each spring, the cranes fly from Mexico and the southern part of the United States to Canada and Alaska. In the fall, they again head south. Large numbers of birds make similar round-trips every year. They migrate mainly to find food, better weather conditions, and places to breed and to raise their young.

Perhaps you, like some scientists, have wondered how migrating birds know just when to come and go. Scientists believe that changes in the hours of daylight are the most important signal. As days grow longer in the spring, the increased periods of sunlight cause changes in the birds' bodies. The birds eat more to store fat for fuel. They grow restless. Soon they take off for their summer homes. The same thing happens in the fall, when days start getting shorter. Changes in the weather and a shrinking food supply may also help the birds know when it's time to move on.

Besides knowing when to migrate, birds seem to know exactly where they're going. Most follow the same routes every year. To find their way, they use their keen senses to respond to a variety of clues. These include landmarks, such as rivers and mountains, and the position of the sun and the stars. Scientists continue to study other factors, as well, that may help the birds navigate on their long journeys.

Underwater Ways

How can people explore deep under the ocean?

Oceans cover nearly three-quarters of the earth's surface. That much water is hard to explore. To spend time beneath the sea, human beings need special equipment. They must be protected from cold, and from the pressure of the surrounding water. The deeper a person goes, the greater the water pressure becomes. Scuba divers rarely go deeper than 200 feet (61 m).*

To expand our abilities to explore underwater, engineers have invented vehicles called submersibles. One such vehicle, *Deep Rover* (right), has mechanical arms and hands for exploring the sea bottom. Below, scientist Sylvia Earle pilots the craft as a scuba diver peers in at her. Air pressure in the submersible stays the same as the pressure at the surface. *Deep Rover* can dive more than 3,000 feet (914 m). Some submersibles have gone much deeper. Experts have also built hundreds of remote-control submersibles that carry no people. Whether controlled from land or piloted in the water, submersibles provide windows to the undersea world.

SYLVIA A. EARLE   *Metric figures in this book have been rounded off.

How do fish breathe?

You probably know that when you breathe, your lungs take in oxygen from the air. Your body cells use the oxygen to provide energy to stay alive. Fish need oxygen just as you do—and for the same reason. Nearly all fish get oxygen from water.

Oxygen is dissolved in water. Fish breathe as water fills their mouths and passes over organs called gills. You can see the gills inside the open mouth of the rainbow trout above. The gills absorb oxygen from the water and transfer it to the rest of the body.

Here's what happens when most kinds of fish breathe. Water flows through the fish's open mouth. Its mouth closes, and the water passes over the gills. They are located in pockets in either side of the head. The gills contain leaflike sheets of tissue

called lamellae (luh-MEL-ee). Blood flows through the lamellae. As it does, it absorbs oxygen from the water and releases carbon dioxide as waste. Blood vessels send the oxygen to all the cells in the fish's body. The water passes out of the fish's body through gill openings on both sides of its head.

Usually, this breathing process provides the fish with enough oxygen. But sometimes fish rise to the surface and gulp a little air. You may have seen goldfish do this. It's usually a sign that the oxygen supply in the water is low. The cause may be decaying food or a bowl that is too small. As food decays, it uses up oxygen. Try changing the water more often or feeding the fish less. You may also need to use a larger bowl.

Manes and Beards

Why do male lions have manes?

This yawning lion's shaggy mane grew because of the influence of a male hormone called testosterone (teh-STAHS-tuh-rohn). Lions, however, aren't the only creatures to have hormones. You have hormones, too. These hormones, or chemical messengers, take charge of your growth and development. In humans, testosterone causes a beard to grow. Testosterone permits some male birds to grow colorful feathers. In male deer, the hormone controls the growth of antlers.

Adult male lions are the only members of the cat family to have manes. Young males may have a little hair around their heads. Not until they are mature adults, however, do they grow full, bushy manes on their heads and necks. This happens when they are about five years old.

Zoologists—scientists who study animals— think that a lion's mane has several purposes. A large mane on a lion may impress other males, by making the animal look bigger, stronger, and more threatening than he really is. The mane may help protect the lion's neck during fights with other males. And the mane shows the lion's maleness— just as a beard does on a man.

JEFFRY W. MYERS/WEST STOCK

HANS REINHARD/BRUCE COLEMAN LTD.

Why don't young boys grow beards?

When these two boys finish playing, they won't have any hair on their faces. But that won't be because they gave themselves a close shave. Their razors, of course, have no blades.

Not until after the boys reach puberty (PYOO-bert-ee) will they begin to grow beards. Puberty is the stage of life when a child starts to become an adult. During puberty, the brain causes an increase in the production of certain hormones. These hormones move through the blood and tell the body to produce other hormones, including testosterone.

As boys begin to grow into men, their bodies make increased amounts of testosterone. Females produce this hormone, too. But males produce about 20 times more than females. Eventually, testosterone will cause changes in the bodies of the boys. They will become more muscular. Their voices will deepen. They will grow hair on parts of their bodies. And beards will begin to grow on their faces—first on their upper lips, later on their chins and cheeks. Then they'll have to put blades in their razors to get a close shave.

One of a Kind

Why are all fingerprints different?

Just as no two people look *exactly* alike, no two people—even identical twins—have exactly the same fingerprints. Fingerprints form while a baby is inside its mother's body.

The skin on your fingertips and thumbs and on your palms resembles the skin on the soles of your feet. It is thicker than the skin on other parts of your body. It has ridges, or raised areas, and valleys, the spaces between the ridges.

The ridges and valleys on your fingers and thumbs form individual fingerprints. Some ridges

JANET F. DWYER/FIRST LIGHT (BOTH)

may divide to form forked lines. Other ridges may end abruptly. Still others may be so short that they look like dots. The arrangement of these ridge characteristics makes your fingerprints and thumbprints different from those of any other person.

Although all fingerprints are different, they do fall into three basic categories: arches, loops, and circular patterns called whorls. You may have inherited patterns like those of your parents, but you have your own versions of them.

Because no two fingerprints are exactly alike, they are a foolproof means of identifying a person. When a finger or a thumb touches a surface, it may leave behind a one-of-a-kind mark. Some prints—those left by a dirty hand, for example—are visible. Others—those made by perspiration or body oil—are hidden or partly hidden. As the body perspires, moisture accumulates on the ridges on the fingertips and thumbs. Body oil may also accumulate there. That happens if a person touches oily parts of the body, such as the face or the scalp. When the person then touches an object, such as a car window, the ridges leave marks on the glass. The prints will become visible when fingerprint powder is brushed over them.

The police officer at left is brushing a stolen car with fingerprint powder. After prints appeared, he lifted the powdered patterns with tape. The prints were then photographed against the car's red hood (below). The information written next to them helps police keep accurate records. If the prints match any of those on file with law-enforcement agencies, the police will know who probably stole the car.

Why does each snowflake have a different shape?

No one has ever recorded finding two identical snowflakes. Scientists say it's extremely unlikely that anyone ever will. Snowflakes are actually crystals of snow that have clumped together while falling. Each snow crystal—a kind of ice crystal—has a shape of its own. As it falls, it passes through many layers of air. Its size and shape keep changing. It may grow, partly melt, or partly evaporate.

On this page, you see a collection of photographs of snow crystals. Does it surprise you that they all don't resemble the lacy stars children often cut out? The starlike crystals on this page are called dendritic (den-DRIT-ik) crystals. Snow crystals come in many other basic shapes as well. Here, you see examples of six shapes. The drawings below identify the kinds of crystals in the photographs.

The next time it snows, catch some crystals on a piece of dark cloth and look at them through a magnifying glass. They all won't be so nearly perfect as the ones shown here, but they all will be different.

| Needle | Dendritic Crystal | Column | Capped Column | Bullet | Bullet Cluster |

RICHARD C. WALTERS   MARVIN J. FRYER (ART)

Green Machines

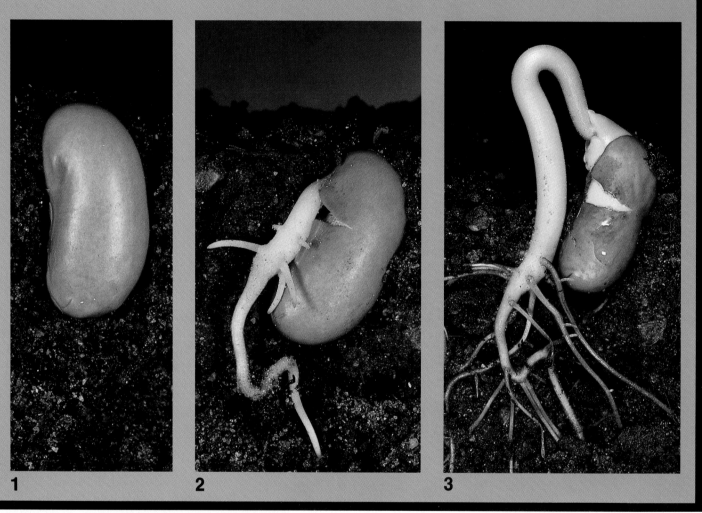

Why does a sprouting seed always send its roots down and its stem up?

A seed has no right-side-up position. When you plant it, you drop it into the soil and cover it. No matter how the seed lies there, when it sprouts, the roots will grow down, and the stem will grow up.

The series of photographs above shows a red kidney bean sprouting. **1)** Buried in soil, the bean—which is a seed—remains inactive for a time. Water and the right temperature will encourage its growth. The water seeps into its tough protective coating and softens it.

2) Soon, the coating bursts. A tiny pale root starts to grow—downward. The root is responding to the pull of gravity. It is growing toward the center of the earth. Experts call this movement positive geotropism (jee-AH-truh-piz-uhm).

3) As the root system develops, a hook-shaped stem starts to grow. The hook pushes up through the soil, moving away from the pull of gravity. The action is known as negative geotropism. When the hook breaks through the surface, the sprout will start to straighten out. Then the plant will head for the sun, growing toward light. This movement is called phototropism (foh-TAH-truh-piz-uhm).

There is one place where sprouts won't behave as they ought to: in space. Without gravity, seeds grow in all directions.

How can you grow different kinds of fruit on the same tree?

Apple lovers can triple their pleasure with a tree like the one below. Dangling from its branches are Golden Delicious apples, green Granny Smith apples, and red McIntosh apples.

Such trees don't grow naturally. Fruit growers create them by a process called grafting. In grafting, a grower joins two or more plants to form a single living plant. An apple tree may produce several different kinds of apples through grafting.

Grafting works only with trees or shrubs that are related to one another. An apple cannot be grafted onto a peach tree. But the bud of any tree with a stone fruit, such as a peach, an apricot, or a plum, can be grafted onto any other stone-fruit tree.

Fruit growers don't graft plants just to produce unusual-looking trees. Grafting has advantages. It is faster than growing new trees from seed. It allows a fruit grower to cultivate trees that produce different varieties of high-quality fruit. A graft can also repair a damaged tree.

Below, you can see the steps involved in one method of grafting, called bud grafting.

1 A small, T-shaped slit is cut in the bark of the rooted stem, called the stock. The stock will receive a bud from the tree the grower wants to graft.

2 The bud is slipped into the cut made on the stock. The parts of both plants that carry food and water must lie against each other. That way, the bud will receive food and water from the stock.

3 The slit in the stock is wrapped snugly with special tape. When the bud begins to grow, the tape will be removed.

WILLIAM COULTER

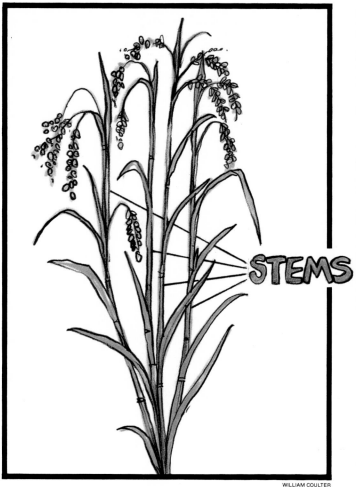

How do plants drink?

Does the photograph at right look a little like Spider-man's face? Actually, it is a slice from a stem of a rice plant, the type of plant in the drawing. The slice is shown greatly enlarged. A photographer added a stain to the slice to make it glow. Scientists use such photographs to study the veins in plant stems.

Within a plant, water travels through a network of veins called the vascular system. The plant absorbs water from the soil. Tiny parts of its roots, called root hairs, take in the water. Each root hair allows water and some minerals to pass through it into the plant. The water then is drawn into the vascular system. Two kinds of tissue—xylem (ZY-luhm) and phloem (FLOW-em)—make up the system. Xylem takes water up from the roots and delivers it to every part of the plant. Phloem carries food, made in the leaves, to other parts of the plant. In the photograph, Spider-man's forehead is the phloem. His eyes, nose, and mouth are the xylem.

To see a plant's vascular system in action, take a stalk of celery and trim the bottom with a knife. Place the stalk in a glass of water to which you have added some food coloring. Overnight, the xylem should carry the coloring to the leaves.

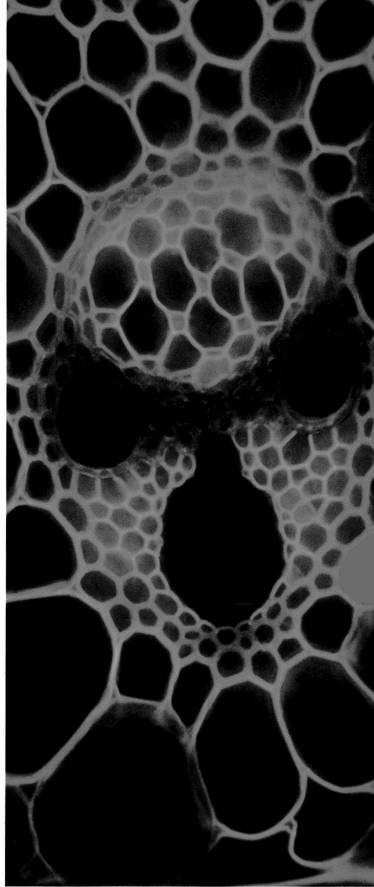

Why don't cactuses have leaves?

Most cactuses live in deserts, where little rain falls. The plants have gradually stopped growing leaves. Leaves allow a plant's water supply to evaporate. When rain falls, plants absorb extra water. In leafy plants, this extra water seeps out through tiny pores in the leaves. Cactuses store the water.

Scientists believe that many areas that are now desert were not so dry millions of years ago. Cactuses had leaves then. A few kinds still do, though the leaves usually are tiny. The cactuses don't depend on leaves for food making, as most plants do.

Cactuses make food in their stems. That's why the stems are green. They contain the green food-making substance chlorophyll (KLOR-uh-fill).

Cactus stems do another important job. They serve as storage tanks for water. A saguaro (suh-WAHR-uh or suh-WAHR-oh), the kind of cactus shown below, has a stem that expands like an accordion. A large saguaro can hold tons of water.

STEPHEN J. KRASEMANN/DRK PHOTO (BOTH)

How do desert animals survive long dry spells without drinking water?

A desert tortoise gets set to chomp on a plant (above). The plant provides not only food, but also some of the water the tortoise needs.

When rain falls in a desert, tortoises and most other desert animals may take a drink. Since it doesn't rain often, however, they may have to live for months without drinking again. When the land is dry, plant-eaters like the tortoise find water in grasses, shrubs, and other plants. Meat-eaters use fluids from the animals they hunt and eat.

Desert animals are well suited to heat and to lack of water. The desert tortoise lives in dry parts of the southwestern United States and Mexico. Its hard shell and leathery skin help keep the water in its body from evaporating. The small kangaroo rat of North America feeds mostly on dry seeds. Like other animals, it produces water as it digests its food. The tiny creature can survive on this water. It may never need a drink at all.

To stay cool and save moisture, most desert animals retreat to dens, burrows, and other shady places during the hottest part of the day. In the cool evening or early morning, they search for food.

Turn, Turn, Turn

KEN SHERMAN/BRUCE COLEMAN INC.

Why does hair turn gray or white as people grow older?

One day, the hair of this eight-year-old boy may be as white as his grandfather's. As people grow older, their hair may turn gray or white.

Some people have hair that begins losing its color at an early age. Their parents' or grandparents' hair probably did the same. Early graying tends to run in families.

Hair outside the scalp consists of dead cells. A person's hair color starts beneath the surface of the scalp, where the hair grows. Each hair is rooted in a narrow pocket called a hair follicle. Certain cells inside the root of the hair produce a dark pigment, or coloring substance. This pigment, known as melanin (MEL-uh-nuhn), is deposited into each hair. A person's hair color depends mainly on the amount, type, and distribution of the melanin.

As people age, the number of melanin-producing cells usually decreases. Many of the cells that remain produce less melanin or stop producing it altogether. Then hair turns gray or white.

Why does the clear part of an egg turn white when it is fried?

Do you prefer your fried eggs sunny-side up, like the one below, or over easy? Whatever your preference, you've probably noticed an odd thing happening as an egg fries. The clear part of the egg thickens and turns white. This thickening process is called coagulation (co-ag-yuh-LAY-shun).

Here's how coagulation works. The white of the egg is made up of widely spaced molecules of protein. In an uncooked egg, these molecules contain a lot of moisture.

When an egg begins to fry, heat gives the molecules extra energy. They begin to stretch out, move around, and bump into one another. As they do, they become tightly linked. This linking of molecules is actually coagulation. As the egg white coagulates, moisture that is squeezed from the molecules evaporates. Light rays cannot pass through the thicker material. The once clear substance now looks white—and it lives up to its name.

CECILE BRUNSWICK/PETER ARNOLD, INC.

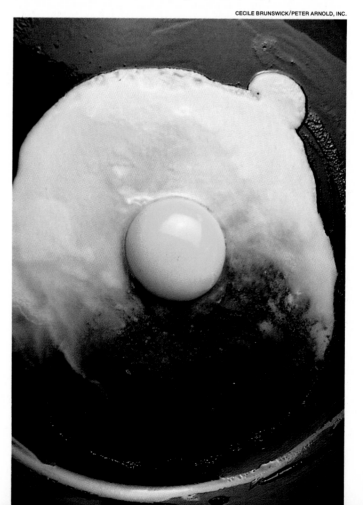

Why do leaves turn color and drop off in autumn?

Every autumn, many kinds of trees put on an eye-popping show. Their leaves turn yellow, orange, red, and purple, painting the landscape.

The leaves that turn yellow and orange in autumn have contained yellow and orange pigments all along. But in summer you cannot see the colors. A stronger color—the green pigment chlorophyll (KLOR-uh-fill)—hides them.

Chlorophyll helps leaves perform their main function: producing sugar. The chlorophyll absorbs sunlight, which serves as energy for making the sugar. During the summer, the leaves send the sugar to other parts of the tree, to be used for growth or stored.

As autumn arrives, shorter days, lower temperatures, and other factors trigger changes in the tree. Gradually, the chlorophyll decays. Without chlorophyll, yellow or orange pigments become visible in some leaves. In other leaves, new pigments form. They turn the leaves red or purple.

The trees that undergo such a change are deciduous (dih-SIHJ-oo-wus), that is, they periodically lose their leaves. As a leaf turns color, it develops a new layer of cells at the base of its stem. The new layer blocks off the leaf from the tree. Soon the leaf falls to the ground.

To survive the winter, the tree enters a dormant, or resting, period. It lives on stored sugar until the following spring, when new leaves begin the sugar-making process again.

Why do some birds have bright feathers?

The patterns and colors of a peacock's feather shine in the sunlight (below). Their message? "Look at me." The male bird's fan of colorful feathers is an advertisement to attract females, called peahens. Peahens don't wear gorgeous patterns of brilliant colors. Their feathers are much duller looking. Among most kinds of birds, males look more colorful than females. The males show off their bright feathers to attract mates and to warn other males to stay away. Females often have special coloring designed to help them hide. For example, many female ducks have brownish feathers streaked with dull colors matching the plants near their nests. When the females sit on the nests, they blend into the background. Enemies are less likely to spot the camouflaged female ducks.

TERRY DOMICO/EARTH IMAGES

CRAIG AURNESS/WEST LIGHT (ABOVE AND BELOW, RIGHT)

Why are flowers so colorful?

From the air, fields of bright flowers (above) look like a multicolored flag. Scientists think their shades and shapes may have a purpose. They may announce to animal pollinators that the flowers have something to offer: food in the form of nectar and pollen.

The color of a flower may give a useful signal to insects searching for food. For example, many white, pink, and yellow flowers send a message that their nectar is especially easy to reach.

The flowers at right display some of the colors that attract bees. Bees are especially attracted to white flowers. The insects, however, cannot see the

color red. Red flowers often attract many kinds of butterflies and birds.

Frequently, colorful petals are arranged in a way that draws insects and birds to the centers of the flowers. That's where the pollen is found.

Flowers often use colorful advertising in somewhat the same way that male birds use colorful feathers to attract mates. A flower's colors attract certain insects and birds, which pick up pollen and carry it to other flowers. This process, called pollination, is necessary for many plants to produce seeds. The seeds then become another generation of flowers in another season.

Two Tricks

Why do certain plants move when you touch them?

Left undisturbed, the feathery leaf sections of the sensitive plant lie open (left). Two rows of tiny leaflets make up each of these sections. If touched lightly, the leaflets will fold together (below). This shrubby plant, a kind of mimosa (muh-MOH-suh), grows wild in the southern United States and in other warm climates. Its leaves contain special cells that swell with water. These cells keep the leaflets open. When part of a leaf is touched or disturbed, water suddenly moves into spaces between the cells. The leaflets close. Soon water returns to the cells, and the leaflets reopen.

Scientists are not sure if this behavior has a purpose. It may protect the sensitive plant from plant-eating animals. A hungry animal that brushes against the plant may be tricked in two ways: As the leaflets fold, the plant may become harder to recognize, and the folded leaflets expose sharp prickles.

TERRY DOMICO/EARTH IMAGES (BOTH)

How and why do chameleons and anoles change color?

If you think you see four different kinds of lizards on this page, you've been fooled. There are only two kinds here: the chameleon (kuh-MEEL-yuhn) in the two pictures above and the green anole (uh-NO-lee) in the two pictures at right. Both change color.

Chameleons, slow-moving reptiles, have long, sticky tongues, bulging eyes, and tails that can grasp things. Most live in Africa and on the nearby island of Madagascar. Chameleons turn many shades of green, yellow, and brown. Some may turn white or black. A chameleon's colors may be solid, or they may form patterns.

The green anole is sometimes called the American chameleon because it too changes color. It turns shades ranging from green to brown. However, this slender, fast-moving North American lizard is not a chameleon at all.

In both chameleons and anoles, a dark substance called melanin (MEL-uh-nuhn) determines color. Melanin occurs in certain cells in a lizard's skin. When the melanin stays tightly packed in the cells, the lizard appears light in color. When the melanin spreads out, the lizard becomes darker.

Studies have shown that many things affect the color of chameleons and anoles. For example, if a lizard is disturbed or if the air temperature changes, the animal may turn a different color, or its pattern may lighten or darken.

Scientists are not sure whether color change serves any purpose for the reptiles. It may help regulate the animals' body temperatures. Or it may confuse their enemies. Scientists do know, however, that chameleons and anoles cannot—as many people think—change color on purpose to match their backgrounds.

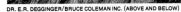

What a Breeze!

Why do kites fly?

Whether they have simple shapes or fancy faces, kites are lightweights. However, kites still weigh more than air. They need help from the wind to soar.

If you hold a kite parallel to the ground, it probably won't go anywhere. But if you tilt the kite upward on a windy day, you give the wind a broad surface to push against. Soon you'll feel a tug on your string. The tightly stretched string will hold the kite against the upward push of the wind. The air pressure on the underside of the kite becomes greater than the pressure above it, forcing the kite upward. This force is called lift. If the wind dies down for a time, you can still launch your kite. Run with the kite until it starts to rise. Keep the string tight. The moving kite disturbs the air, creating lift.

If you have a kite with an unusual shape, other forces may act on it as well, depending on how the wind circulates around its surfaces. Whatever its shape, once your kite is aloft, it should stay there—as long as its design is sound and the wind is steady.

How does a parachute work?

Thousands of feet above the earth, a sky diver jumps from an airplane. Soon he is falling at more than 100 miles an hour (161 km/h). When he wants to open his main parachute, he releases a small pilot parachute. The small chute is attached to the top of the main parachute. As the pilot parachute fills with air, it tugs on the main parachute. Within seconds the main parachute unfolds. It provides a huge surface for air to press against. Air resisting the falling chute slows the jumper's fall.

The parachute you see here has the newest shape, a rectangle. This design gives the parachutist greater control over his speed and movements than the old umbrella-shaped chute did. By adjusting the chute, the jumper can slow down and make a gentle landing right side up.

CHARLES KREBS

Why do both birds and bicyclists follow closely behind one another?

Birds and bicyclists play follow-the-leader for good reason. Staying behind helps them move ahead.

Does that sound impossible? It isn't. The leader of a flying flock and the leader of a pedaling pack have something in common. Both have the toughest job in the group. The leader has to slice through the air, which resists. As the leader moves ahead, disturbed air spreads behind in a V shape, like the waves behind a boat. Air currents in the V form whirlpools. The second bird or cyclist gets an extra push from the whirlpools—and so on down the line.

Followers benefit from air currents in another way, too. Moving air squeezed into a small space speeds up. If a racing cyclist passes another racer closely, or if a bird passes close to another bird, the air between them helps move the passer along.

Geese (left) and other birds that travel long distances often follow the leader. Only highly trained bicyclists, like those below, have the skill to ride safely in the same way. Never try riding closely behind another bicycle or any other vehicle. Painful accidents can happen very quickly.

ROBERT P. CARR/BRUCE COLEMAN INC.

DAVID BARNES/APERTURE PHOTOBANK

Why does a boomerang return to you after you throw it?

If you throw a boomerang properly, you won't lose it. It will travel in a circle and come back to you. The secret lies in two things: its shape and how it is thrown.

Most modern boomerangs have two arms. Each arm is curved on the top and flat on the bottom, like an airplane wing. The shape of the curve produces one rounded edge and one flat edge. There's an important difference between the shape of a boomerang arm and the shape of an airplane wing, however. On an airplane, the rounded edges of both wings face forward. The rounded edges of a boomerang's arms face in opposite directions. As the boomerang spins, its design creates unequal air pressure. The pressure pushes it to one side.

To throw a boomerang properly, launch it so that it spins vertically, like a bicycle wheel. This gives it an extra push. Air always flows faster over the arm on top. That arm slices *forward* on each spin. The bottom arm slices *backward*, which cuts down its speed. The difference in speeds makes the air pressure on the arms even more unequal. The whirling boomerang starts to make a circle, just as your bicycle does when you unbalance it by leaning to one side. If the throw was a good one, the boomerang will come full circle and land at your feet.

How does an airplane fly on automatic pilot?

Shortly after takeoff, the pilot of a jet airplane turns a series of knobs and moves a lever in the cockpit. The pilot has set the course and put the airplane on automatic pilot. You might think the airplane is headed for disaster, but it isn't. With the plane set on automatic pilot, the passengers will have a safer, more comfortable ride.

An automatic pilot, or autopilot, is an electrical device. It helps the pilot of an airplane control the speed, altitude, and course of the aircraft. The autopilot runs by gyroscope (JEYE-ruh-skope). In its simplest form, a gyroscope consists of a rapidly spinning wheel mounted in a special frame. Once the wheel starts spinning, it holds its position—no matter how much everything around it moves.

The pilot sets the airplane's gyroscopes in the direction the airplane should go. The gyroscopes then keep track of the plane's position and movements. If the airplane moves away from the course set by the pilot, the gyroscopes send electrical signals to small motors. The motors do what the pilot would do,

only faster. They adjust the controls in the cockpit to put the plane back on course.

The cockpit controls move hinged sections of the wings and tail. These sections are called control surfaces. Changing the angle of any control surface changes the way air pushes on the plane. That makes the plane move in one of three ways. The drawings at right show how various control surfaces affect airplane motion. Elevators, in the tail, make the nose go up or down (pitch). This causes the plane to climb or dive. Ailerons (AY-luh-rahns), in the wings, tilt the plane from side to side (roll). The rudder, in the tail, turns the plane left or right (yaw).

An automatic pilot makes many tiny changes in the positions of the control surfaces. It steers a steadier course than any human can. An autopilot also frees the pilot to watch over other instruments. Once an airplane is in the air, the human pilot may not have to touch the controls for hours. At any time, the human can give the autopilot new instructions or turn it off and take control.

JIM LARSEN/WEST STOCK

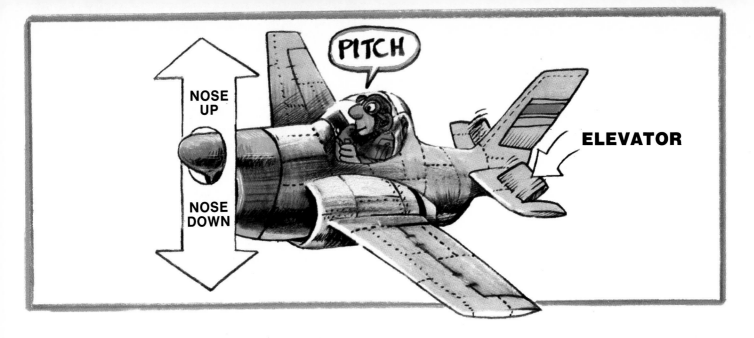

47

How does a boat sail toward the wind?

It's easy to see how a sailboat sails with the wind behind it. The wind pushes against the sails, driving the boat forward. But a sailboat, even this toy one, can also sail in the direction from which the wind blows. The boat can't go straight into the wind, but it can sail toward the wind. It works this way.

The sails split the oncoming wind in two. The wind blowing over the outer curves of the sails travels farther, therefore faster. The faster wind speed causes the wind at the sails' outer curves to have less pressure than wind at the inner curves. The difference in pressure moves the boat forward.

You might think the boat would move sideways. It does—but only slightly. The underwater part of the boat is designed to resist most sideward pressure and change it into forward motion.

How does a Hovercraft travel?

The coast guard rescue craft below isn't plowing through the water. It's riding on a cushion of air. A Hovercraft gets its name from the way it hovers, or floats, just above the surface. A powerful fan inside the top of the Hovercraft sucks in air. The fan forces the air down into a flexible skirt around the bottom of the hull. As the trapped air pushes against the surface, it lifts the craft. Propellers on top move it forward or backward.

Because the craft doesn't have to push through water, it moves faster than do boats with engines of the same size. When the water is rough, the cushion of air smooths out the ride. But a Hovercraft doesn't always move over water. It also travels on land.

CHUCK O'REAR/WEST LIGHT

PAUL KOTZ/WEST STOCK

CANADIAN COAST GUARD

RESCUE   GARDE CÔTIÈRE

Hot Stuff

What makes a fire burn?

During a winter camping trip in the Rocky Mountains, three youngsters warm their hands over a wood fire. Even though the snow on the ground is frozen, the flames burn bright and hot. That's because the fuel the campers used to build the fire reached a temperature called the kindling temperature. For wood, this temperature is about 500°F (260°C). Other fuels burst into flame at different temperatures—some lower, some higher.

To make a fire, you need fuel. You must heat the fuel to its kindling temperature. You also need a good supply of oxygen. When the chemicals that make up the fuel unite with the oxygen, a series of chemical reactions takes place. Those chemical reactions, called combustion, produce the flames we see and the heat we feel. Take away any one of the three necessities—fuel, oxygen, or kindling temperature—and the fire will go out.

If you accidentally drop a lighted match on paper or leaves, you may start a blaze. But if you drop a match on a stone walk or a brick patio, nothing will happen. Why not? Stone, brick, and many other materials are fireproof. Oxygen cannot combine with these materials, so they cannot burn.

CHUCK O'REAR/WEST LIGHT

ANTHONY HOWARTH/INT'L STOCK PHOTOGRAPHY

How can a laser cut through metal?

Sparks fly as a laser cuts sharp teeth into a blade for a circular saw (above). It takes the laser only two minutes to cut each blade.

The light a laser produces is concentrated into a single beam. Ordinary light spreads out in all directions as it travels away from its source. The narrow beam of laser light travels in only one direction. It hardly spreads out at all. As a result, a powerful laser can send a huge amount of energy to a tiny spot. That energy produces tremendous heat. A laser beam can raise the temperature of a substance at the rate of nearly two *trillion* degrees Fahrenheit (about a trillion degrees Celsius) a second.

Properly focused at close range (right), a certain kind of laser beam becomes a high-speed cutting tool. It simply turns metal into vapor. The only part of the metal to vaporize, however, is the part that is touched by the beam of light.

Because a laser beam can be focused to a pinpoint, lasers can do jobs that demand great accuracy. Workers use them to put together tiny computer chips. Surgeons use them to operate on parts of the body as delicate as the eye.

How is glass made from sand?

When you hold a drinking glass in your hand, you're actually holding sand, with a few added chemicals. The ingredients have been transformed by the power of heat. Here is what happens. A glassmaker heats the sand and chemicals in a large furnace. Very high heat is needed to transform these ingredients into a transparent substance that can be shaped and hardened. When the mixture reaches a temperature of about 2,700°F (1,482°C), it melts. It changes into a thick, syrupy liquid. As the liquid cools, it slowly hardens and becomes glass.

The beakers in the photograph at left contain sand, lime, and soda ash, a chemical similar to baking soda. These are the raw materials needed to make the most common kind of glass. Chunks of colored glass surround the beakers. Added ingredients—usually powdered metals—give glass its wide range of colors. In the background of the photograph, some workers stand near a red-hot furnace. They will reheat glass for a special effect. The glass they are using will turn from clear to milky white.

Glass must be shaped before it hardens. Below, a craftsman called a gaffer trims away excess glass to form the rim of a goblet. He works near a furnace so he can keep the glass heated as he shapes it.

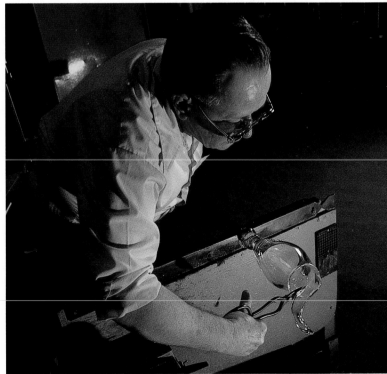

Sounds, Sights, Signals

How do cellular telephones work?

"Hello, Bryan. I have to meet with one more customer before I head for home. Would you just pop the casserole into the oven for dinner, please?"

The driver below is talking to her son. He's at home; she's in her car. With her eyes on the road and her attention on driving, she speaks to him on a cellular car telephone. Her call is carried by radio waves, as are radio and television programs. When the driver placed her call, radio waves traveled from her car to an antenna atop a nearby station. The station has a receiver and a transmitter. When the station received the signals from her phone, it transmitted them through special telephone lines to a mobile-telephone switching office. At the switching

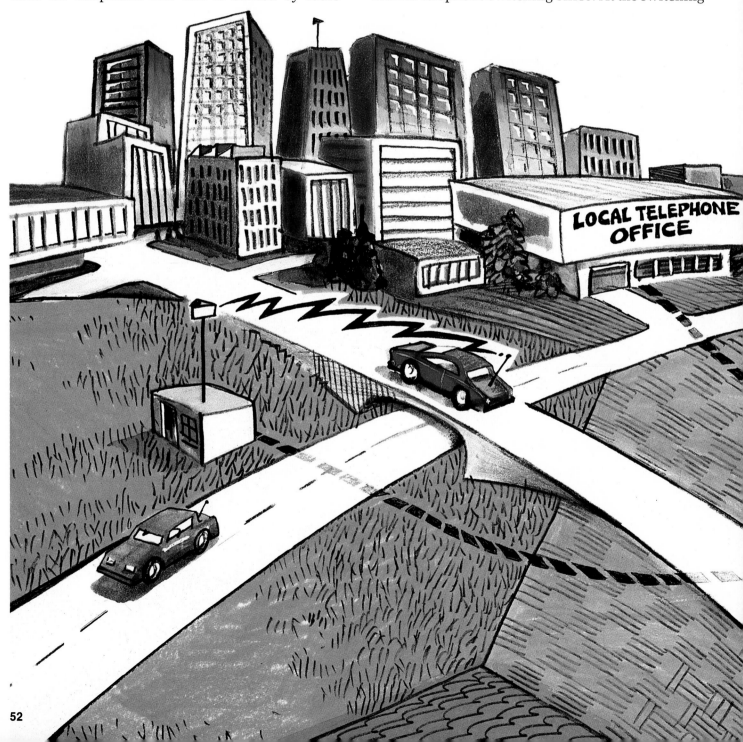

LOCAL TELEPHONE OFFICE

office, a computer connected the call to the regular telephone lines. Because the driver's calls are connected to the regular lines, she can speak to any telephone in the world.

Experts say that by 1990, two and a half million people in the United States may be using cellular car telephones. So far, only the areas in and around large cities have systems for cellular telephones. These areas are divided into sections called cells. Each cell has its own station.

A cell may measure from 1 to 16 miles (1⅔–26 km) across. If you were to outline the cells, you would see a pattern something like the one shown here.

While this driver uses her car telephone, the computer in the main switching office keeps track of the call. As her car nears the edge of one cell, the radio signals from her telephone start to fade. The computer switches the call over to the next cell station. The driver must stay within the cellular system to use her phone.

Today's cellular telephone consists of more than the hand-held piece you see in the drawing. The woman also has a small box of electronic equipment in the trunk and an antenna on her car.

Engineers are constantly reducing the size of cellular-phone parts. Some portable cellular telephones are small enough to fit in briefcases. Few people, as yet, own these. Some day, say engineers, you'll be able to wear a cellular telephone on your wrist, just like a watch.

WILLIAM COULTER

MOBILE-TELEPHONE SWITCHING OFFICE

How does a home video system work?

You don't need to be a famous actor to see yourself on TV. You just need some special equipment.

With a video camera, a portable recorder unit, and a TV set, you can make your own movie and watch it on TV. That's just what the youngsters in the cartoons are doing.

With a video camera and a portable recorder unit, the girl records the image and the voice of her stilt-walking friend. The image and sound go onto a magnetic tape in a video cassette inside the recorder unit. The youngsters then take the recorder indoors. They hook up the recorder to their TV set, rewind the tape, and set the controls on PLAY.

When the tape plays back, the recorder sends electronic signals to the TV. The TV receives and displays the signals. The children see the recorded picture and hear the sound.

Some home video systems have another box called a tuner/timer. Sometimes this serves as a miniature TV transmitter, taking the video signal from a camera or a recorder and sending the signal to the TV set. Once a recording has been made, the video cassette will store the image and sound. The cassette can be played again and again.

54

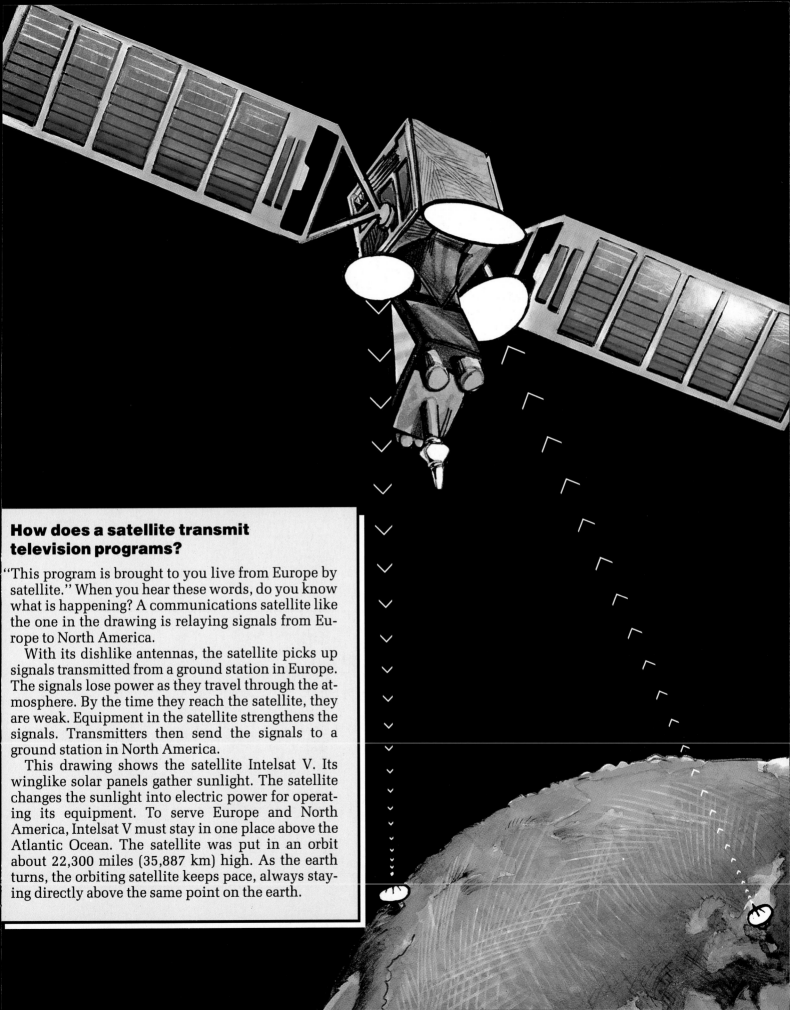

How does a satellite transmit television programs?

"This program is brought to you live from Europe by satellite." When you hear these words, do you know what is happening? A communications satellite like the one in the drawing is relaying signals from Europe to North America.

With its dishlike antennas, the satellite picks up signals transmitted from a ground station in Europe. The signals lose power as they travel through the atmosphere. By the time they reach the satellite, they are weak. Equipment in the satellite strengthens the signals. Transmitters then send the signals to a ground station in North America.

This drawing shows the satellite Intelsat V. Its winglike solar panels gather sunlight. The satellite changes the sunlight into electric power for operating its equipment. To serve Europe and North America, Intelsat V must stay in one place above the Atlantic Ocean. The satellite was put in an orbit about 22,300 miles (35,887 km) high. As the earth turns, the orbiting satellite keeps pace, always staying directly above the same point on the earth.

Sky Sights

Why does the setting sun sometimes appear to change shape?

The setting sun at left seems to be flattened. The setting sun below spreads out at the bottom. Both are mirages—images that fool your eyes.

Mirages occur when light rays pass through layers of air that have differing densities—thicknesses—and differing temperatures. The rays are refracted, or bent, in unusual ways.

You may see a flattened sun like the one at left when air becomes heated at the earth's surface and is cooler just above the surface. These changes in air temperature affect the density of the air. Cool air is denser than hot air. When rays from the sun meet with sudden changes in the density of the air layers, they are refracted. You see the bent rays as a mirage. The brilliant colors result from the scattering of the light rays as they are bending.

The mirage below is called a double image. It occurred when the sun-warmed water heated the lower layers of a mass of much cooler air. The heat caused those lower layers to become less dense than the cooler air above. As light rays sped from the cool layers to water-heated layers, the light waves were refracted sharply away from the water to form the twin image. The sun appears lower than it would ordinarily. Below it you see an upside-down image of part of the sun.

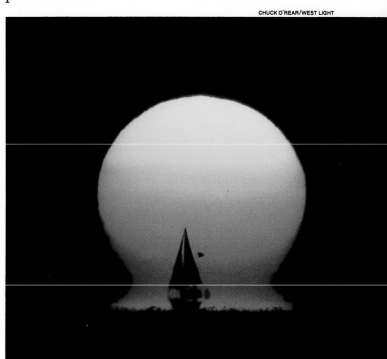

EXPLORER/JEAN-PAUL NACIVET

Why is the sky blue?

For the sun's rays to reach the earth, they must pass through the atmosphere. What happens there makes the sky look blue to you.

Pure sunlight, which appears white, is actually made up of all the colors of the rainbow. The blue and violet light waves are the shortest. The red and orange ones are the longest. As rays of white light approach the earth, some rays bump into molecules of air and particles of dust in the atmosphere. The collision causes some light waves in the rays to scatter in many directions. The short blue and violet waves scatter the most, spreading all over the sky. These scattered waves make the sky appear blue. Normally, the longer waves continue on toward earth. Pollution, however, can scatter these waves.

In a blue sky, the sun looks yellow. Light coming from the sun lacks some of the blue and violet light waves. They have scattered. Sunlight is a combination of the remaining colors.

To see how light scatters, stir a few drops of milk into a jar filled with water. Shine a flashlight through the jar. The milk works like the particles in the atmosphere. The flashlight serves as the sun. The milk will scatter blue and violet light waves from the flashlight. Like the sky, the liquid will look blue.

Why does the moon rise at different times during the year?

The moon only seems to rise. It is passing by as the earth rotates on its axis. Like the sun, the moon appears to move westward across the sky. Actually, it moves eastward. It fools your eyes because of its travel time. It takes the moon about $29\frac{1}{2}$ days to orbit the earth. That is much greater than the time it takes the earth to rotate—24 hours. When the moon is new—between the earth and the sun—it seems to rise and set with the sun. Soon it drops farther behind in its orbit in relation to the sun. Each day, it rises about 50 minutes later. As it rises later, the moon seems to change shape and size. This is because it reflects the sun from an ever-changing angle. Below, a full moon shines over a village in Canada's Northwest Territories.

DAVID HISER/THE IMAGE BANK

NASA

Why do I see a man in the moon?

Cleopatra saw him. So did Abraham Lincoln. You probably have, too. In fact, the man in the moon has appeared in the night sky to every generation.

The moon has no light of its own. Its rough surface reflects light from the sun. Mountainous regions, called highlands, appear light. Flat plains, called maria (MAHR-ee-uh), look dark. Scattered across both the highlands and the maria are craters left by crashing meteorites. All together, these features form a pattern that resembles a face. You can see the light-and-dark pattern in the photograph of the moon at left.

The moon rotates just once on its axis each time it travels around the earth. That is the reason we always see the same side of the moon—the one that looks like a face.

Water and Light

STEPHEN J. KRASEMANN/DRK PHOTO

Why do I see a rainbow?

A recipe for a rainbow calls for only two basic ingredients: water droplets and sunlight. Rainbows occur when sunlight strikes water droplets in the air.

As light rays pass through the atmosphere, they behave differently, depending on what kinds of objects they bump into. Sometimes a ray of light is reflected, or bounced back. Sometimes it is absorbed. Sometimes it is refracted, or bent. White light—the light you see all around you—is a mixture of colored light. When white light hits a droplet of water in the air at a certain angle, it is refracted. As it bends, it fans out into all the colors of the rainbow.

Although each droplet breaks up light into all its colors, only one color of light is then reflected at an angle to reach your eyes. For a rainbow to appear, many droplets must refract and reflect different colors of light to you.

If light strikes raindrops at a certain angle, two reflections may occur. Then you see a double rainbow like the one above.

Would you like to create your own rainbow? Choose a time when the sun is *not* directly overhead. Stand with the sun at your back. With a garden hose, spray water into the air. Adjust the angle of the mist until bands of color appear.

Why does water act as a mirror?

The waters of a river in California's Yosemite National Park reflect the steep cliffs of El Capitan mountain (right). Light may bounce off any surface, but only smooth, shiny surfaces like this one produce mirror images. This river is nearly still. If a breeze came along, you could probably predict what would happen. This "picture" would dissolve into thousands of ripples and disappear.

When you look around, whatever you see is either producing light or reflecting it. When light from the sun strikes El Capitan, it bounces off the mountain and hits the surface of the river.

The image the light forms in your eye—in this case, a picture of a mountain, trees, and sky—is a mirror image of the scene. In a mirror image, light is reflected off a smooth surface in one direction only. It bounces off the surface at the same angle at which it strikes the surface.

When light hits a rough surface, like a rippling stream or a windswept pond, it is also reflected. But the water movement scatters the light rays. They are reflected at many different angles. Then you do not see a clear image. If light did not sometimes scatter as it hits a surface, you could not read this. You would see your face in this page instead of the words.

The Cloud Crowd

How do clouds form?

Whether fat and puffy or thin and feathery, all clouds are portions of cooled air. Air may cool as it rises from a warm surface, as it flows up a mountain slope, or as it is lifted by another air mass.

All air contains water in the form of a gas called water vapor. Warm air can hold more water vapor molecules than cool air. If the air is cooled to a certain point, the molecules change from a gas to

droplets of water, to crystals of ice, or to a mixture of both. We see these droplets and crystals as clouds. Scientists classify clouds by their appearance, by what they are made of, and by how high in the sky they form.

In the middle of the photograph below, a few wispy cirrus (SIHR-us) clouds float above a long, sloping layer of cirrostratus (sihr-oh-STRATE-us)

clouds. Both kinds of clouds occur at high altitudes, where temperatures are below freezing. Both are made of ice crystals. They may have formed when a layer of warm air drifted above a layer of cooler air.

Like a mound of whipped cream, a thick cumulus (KYOO-myuh-lus) cloud sits atop the mountain on the right. This cloud formed when air currents moved up the mountain and then cooled.

The unusual cloud on the left may remind you of a stack of giant pancakes. It is called *Altocumulus lenticularis* (al-toe-KYOO-myuh-lus len-TIK-yuh-LAIR-us). The word "Altocumulus" describes a cloud at medium altitude with a built-up appearance. "Lenticularis" describes the saucer shapes of the cloud. This kind of cloud sometimes develops when the wind blows over hilly or mountainous surfaces.

Why can you see your breath on a cold day?

Usually your breath is invisible. On many cold days, however, it becomes visible—like the breath of the boy and the rooster below. Every time you exhale on such a day, you create a tiny cloud.

Even when the temperature falls outside, your body temperature usually stays at about 98.6°F (37°C). So the air you breathe out on a cold day is much warmer than the air outside. You can feel the warmth of your breath by holding your hands close to your mouth and exhaling. When your warm breath mixes with cold air outside, water vapor in your breath condenses—changes to water droplets—and a cloud forms. The same thing happens when the water in a teakettle comes to a boil. When water vapor escapes to the cooler air in the room, a tiny cloud forms. Like the cloud from the kettle, a breath cloud soon drifts away and evaporates. But with each new breath, you create another cloud.

THOMAS L. DIETRICH/APERTURE PHOTOBANK

JULIE HABEL/WEST LIGHT

What is fog?

If you've walked through fog, you know what it's like to have your head in the clouds. Fog is simply a cloud at the earth's surface.

Like a cloud in the sky, fog consists of water droplets or ice crystals suspended in the air. That's why your skin feels damp when you walk through fog.

In valleys and other low-lying areas, fog may form on clear nights when the air contains a lot of moisture and the wind is gently blowing. With no clouds to reflect heat back to earth, the ground gives off heat. As heat escapes, the ground cools off. The layer of air near the ground cools off, too. Water vapor in the air condenses, and a thin fog develops (above). It is known as ground fog. Usually, ground fog "burns off" during the late morning as the sun warms the air and the ground.

At right, a thick fog nearly hides the Golden Gate Bridge, in San Francisco, California. Fog forms frequently in that coastal city. Warm, moist air blows across the Pacific Ocean. Near the shore, it passes over a cold ocean current. Then it travels onto the cool land. As the moving air becomes chilled, a thick, blanketlike fog may form along the coast. This kind of fog is sometimes called monsoon fog. Monsoon fogs are thicker and last longer than ground fogs. They often block visibility along coastlines, endangering ships.

Why does snow stay on the tops of mountains year-round?

Snow doesn't always mean wintertime—especially on mountaintops. Some peaks have snow on them all summer, too.

Since the top of a mountain is closer to the sun than its base is, you might have thought the peak would be warmer. Actually, it is the mountain's coldest spot. Here's why. The dense atmosphere near the base of a mountain easily traps the sun's

What creates an ice cave?

If you've ever explored a rock cave, you know it can be chilly and beautiful. An ice cave is even colder and, to many people, more beautiful.

Ice caves look like glittering glass palaces. Light passing through the thick ice makes the walls appear blue. Reflections off the walls of ice set them sparkling like diamonds.

Ice caves form near the foot of a glacier. As the foot of the glacier begins to melt, the water it releases creates streams and channels under the glacier. Soon warm summer air pushes into the channels. The air speeds up the melting process. Eventually, the combined action of water and air hollows out a long cave in the glacier.

Many glacial caves are quite large. The one shown above, in Paradise Glacier, in Washington State, is as wide as a three-car garage. Some parts are three stories high. Rocks and dirt cover the floor. As the glacier inched down Mount Rainier, it picked up this material. Glacial caves can be dangerous to explore. Large sheets of ice often crash from the ceiling. Sudden floods can occur. Amateurs should explore glacial caves only through photographs made by experienced cavers.

warm rays. The higher you go up a mountain, however, the thinner the atmosphere becomes. The thinner the air, the less heat it traps, so the temperature grows colder and colder. On the tops of some mountains, such as Mount Cook, in New Zealand (below), it's cold enough for snow to remain all year long.

The boundary above which snow never melts is called the snow line. Mountains in warm regions have high snow lines. Those where the weather is colder have lower snow lines.

The gradual cooling of the air as you climb a mountain affects plant life. Deciduous (dih-SIHJ-oo-wus) trees, trees that periodically lose their leaves, need warmer weather. They grow near a mountain's base. Stronger evergreens grow higher up. Only the sturdiest plants grow near the snow line.

Energy in the Air

What causes a tornado?

Like a wildly spinning top, a tornado whirls around and around. It produces winds that may reach 250 miles an hour (402 km/h)—the fastest and most violent winds on earth.

Most tornadoes occur in the central and southern parts of the United States. There, in spring and early summer, the right conditions for tornadoes often exist. Cold, heavy air from the north collides with lighter, warm air from the south. The lighter air begins to spin counterclockwise until it is above the colder air. Strong winds called jet streams, located about 5 miles (8 km) above the earth, help suck the lighter air upward. Soon a line of dark thunderclouds forms. At the lower surface of one of these clouds, a funnel-shaped cloud appears. With a hiss, it reaches down to the ground. The hiss changes into a roar. A tornado has begun.

In its early stages, a tornado has a thin funnel. **1**) As it roars across the land, scooping up dirt and rubbish, the funnel grows darker, wider, and stronger. The center of the funnel is like a giant vacuum cleaner. It can pick up automobiles and even railroad cars, and carry them hundreds of feet. **2**) The violently rotating winds rip buildings apart and snap trees as easily as if they were matchsticks. **3**) Within seconds, the tornado moves on. Eventually, it weakens and disappears.

Fortunately, most tornadoes last less than an hour and travel only about 20 miles (32 km). Weather forecasters track them and warn people in their paths. By studying tornadoes, experts hope to learn how to control these powerful storms.

© GENE E. MOORE/PHOTOTAKE (ALL)

How do hurricanes form?

From the ground, a hurricane seems wild and form-less (below). But if you could look down on one from above, you would see that a hurricane has a definite shape: a cloudy swirl.

All hurricanes develop over tropical waters. Those that hit North America usually form over the Atlantic Ocean just north of the Equator in the summer and fall. Layers of warm, moist air rise, then cool and form clouds. The rotation of the earth starts these clouds spinning. Soon, a storm is brewing.

In the Atlantic Ocean, winds often carry the storm west and then north. As it moves, it increases in size and speed. When the winds reach 74 miles an hour (119 km/h), weather forecasters call the storm a hurricane. They begin to broadcast warnings. One of the largest of all storms, a hurricane may extend across 500 miles (805 km). At its center, like the hole in a doughnut, is a calm and sometimes cloud-free area known as the eye. Around the eye, heavy rain falls.

Some hurricanes die at sea. Others roar onto land. There, the furious winds may gust up to 200 miles an hour (322 km/h). They knock down trees and power lines, and rip roofs off houses. They also stir up huge waves or tides called storm surges. These surges, some as tall as a two-story building, sweep across the land. They may wash away people, cars, and even buildings.

Once a hurricane moves onto land, it loses its source of energy—warm, moist air. The winds gradually die down. As the hurricane dissolves into heavy rain, it often produces tornadoes.

What is a waterspout?

The whirling column above looks like a tornado, but it isn't. It's a common waterspout, a frequent sight in the waters near the Florida Keys.

Common waterspouts usually occur above shallow tropical waters during the rainy season. They form when air in developing cumulonimbus (KYOO-myuh-loh-NIM-buhs) clouds whirls downward to the water. The wind picks up water droplets from the air, creating spinning funnels of air and water.

Sometimes much more powerful waterspouts, called tornadic waterspouts, occur. They happen when tornadoes form on the sea or move onto it. Tornadic waterspouts are rarer than common waterspouts. Although common waterspouts have less force than tornadic ones, this windsurfer should beware. A common waterspout packs winds of up to 100 miles an hour (161 km/h).

What causes lightning?

With enough energy to light up thousands of light bulbs, lightning flashes across the sky. Scientists think all lightning forms in thunderclouds. There, water droplets, ice crystals, and dust particles collide. They rub against each other, then split apart. They become energized; that is, they take on negative or positive charges.

The smaller particles develop positive charges. The larger ones take on negative charges. The positive charges are in the middle and upper parts of the cloud. The heavier negative charges drop to the lower part. The cloud then becomes a kind of giant battery, positive at the top and negative at the bottom. Like charges repel, or drive away, one another. Opposite charges attract. The opposite charges in the cloud are attracted to each other. But air is a poor conductor of electricity. It separates the charges and makes it difficult for them to join. When enough opposite charges build up, however, they rush together and meet with a flash. This flash is lightning.

Usually, lightning jumps from one part of a cloud to another. Sometimes, however, it leaps from cloud to cloud. And sometimes it just ends up in the air. About a third of the time, it strikes the earth. Why doesn't lightning hit the ground more often? The thick layer of air between the clouds and the earth usually prevents this from happening.

As lightning blasts through the sky, it heats the air along its path to temperatures as high as 54,000°F (29,982°C). Instantly, the air explodes in a series of waves. You hear these waves as the slow rumble or sharp clap of thunder.

Underground Forces

Why do volcanoes erupt in different ways?

How a volcano erupts depends on what's going on inside the earth. Far below the earth's surface, temperatures are extremely high. In a few places deep underground, rock melts to form a hot, flowing substance called magma. The magma contains dissolved gases. A lot of dissolved gas makes magma thin and runny. Magma that does not have much gas in it is thick and sticky.

Because magma weighs less than the solid rock around it, it gradually rises toward the surface. Sometimes it erupts, forming a volcano. Magma at the earth's surface is called lava. Thin lava gushes out of a volcano as a red-hot liquid. At left, liquid lava and cinders shoot from Kilauea, a volcano on the island of Hawaii. Below, flowing like a river, fiery lava spills rapidly down the side of the volcano.

When thin magma erupts as lava, it releases gas easily. Thick magma traps gas. When the trapped gas finally escapes during an eruption, lava explodes as ash, cinders, and globs of melted rock called bombs. At right, you can see such an eruption at Mount St. Helens. On May 18, 1980, that volcano, in Washington State, erupted with a roar. People could hear the blast from more than 200 miles (322 km) away. What set off such a violent eruption? Magma, under high pressure, moved upward into the volcano. An earthquake triggered the eruption. Billions of fragments of cinders and ash darkened the sky for hundreds of miles.

How can we tap the energy inside the earth?

Instead of burning coal or oil, the power plant below uses geothermal energy, or heat from the earth. People can tap this energy source in places where magma heats underground water.

Underground water lies close to the earth's surface. In some places, magma forms too deep in the earth to heat this water. In other areas, however, magma lies less than 10 miles (16 km) underground. It heats the rock layers around it and any water flowing through them. The water boils and forms steam under great pressure. Sometimes the pressure causes a geyser or a hot spring to form. In other places, the steam escapes through a natural vent called a fumarole (FYOO-muh-role).

To tap the underground steam, engineers drill wells through layers of rock. They put pipes in the wells. Steam rushes through the pipes to the surface. There, machines change the high-pressure steam into electricity.

What causes a geyser?

Whoosh! Steam and hot water shoot from Castle Geyser, in Wyoming's Yellowstone National Park (above). The geyser erupts for a time. Then, suddenly, it stops. When water seeps back underground and heats up, the geyser will erupt again.

To picture a geyser, think of a system of narrow tubes twisting deep into the ground. These tubes, natural channels, descend from an opening at the earth's surface toward red-hot magma below. Rain and melted snow continually trickle into the tubes. Magma heats up rock, which heats water at the bottom of the tube system. The water becomes superheated—heated above the boiling point. However, the weight of the water above it keeps the lower water from boiling. Eventually, the higher water heats up and begins to boil. Rising steam pushes a little of the water out of the opening. This eases the pressure below enough to let the lower water suddenly boil. More steam forms rapidly. A burst of steam and water shoots out of the ground as a geyser.

VOLKER CORELL/SKYLINE FEATURES, INC.

Can scientists predict earthquakes?

The earthquake that struck Coalinga, California, in 1983 took residents like the homeowner above by surprise. That's because scientists cannot yet predict the *exact* spot and time an earthquake will occur. They do know, however, that quakes occur along faults—cracks in the earth's rocky crust. Here, movement of the crust causes built-up energy to be suddenly released. This release of energy is felt as an earthquake. To try to predict where and when a quake will occur, scientists use a variety of sensitive instruments—underground, on the surface, and in space. The instruments measure changes that might signal a coming quake. At right, light from a laser flashes across a fault in California. A mirror will reflect the light back to the laser. If the land shifts, the time it takes the light to make a round-trip changes. Scientists study past earthquakes for patterns of activity that can serve as warning signs. These observations, they believe, are providing keys to more accurate earthquake predictions.

CHUCK O'REAR/WEST LIGHT

Why are the Himalayas so high?

Tops among mountains, the Himalayas of Asia rise higher than any other range in the world. The Himalayas are so high because of the way they were formed and because they are still being uplifted.

To imagine how the Himalayas were formed, think of the earth's continents and ocean floors as pieces of a jigsaw puzzle. These pieces, called plates, make up the earth's crust. Beneath the crust is a thick layer of partly melted rock. In this layer, heat from within the earth produces very slow currents. The currents cause the plates to move.

At one time, a sea separated India from the rest of Asia. The Himalayas began forming when the edge of the plate carrying India started to slide under the plate carrying Asia. This action pushed up part of the ocean floor. India finally collided with Asia 40 to 60 million years ago. The force caused the landmasses to buckle, creating the Himalayan range.

India has continued to push into Asia, thrusting the mountains to their present height during the last 600,000 years. Some earthquakes in Asia may be caused by the ongoing collision.

The Himalayas are gradually being worn down by rain, moving ice, and wind. Most scientists believe, however, that the range is being uplifted faster than it is being worn down.

The cloud-swept mountain at right is Mount Everest, the highest peak in the world. It lies in the Himalayas on the border between Nepal and China. Below, two men pause at its top after weeks of exhausting climbing. The layers of rock now at the top of Mount Everest, 5½ miles (9 km) above sea level, once lay at the bottom of the sea.

PAT MORROW/FIRST LIGHT

BILL O'CONNOR/PETER ARNOLD, INC.

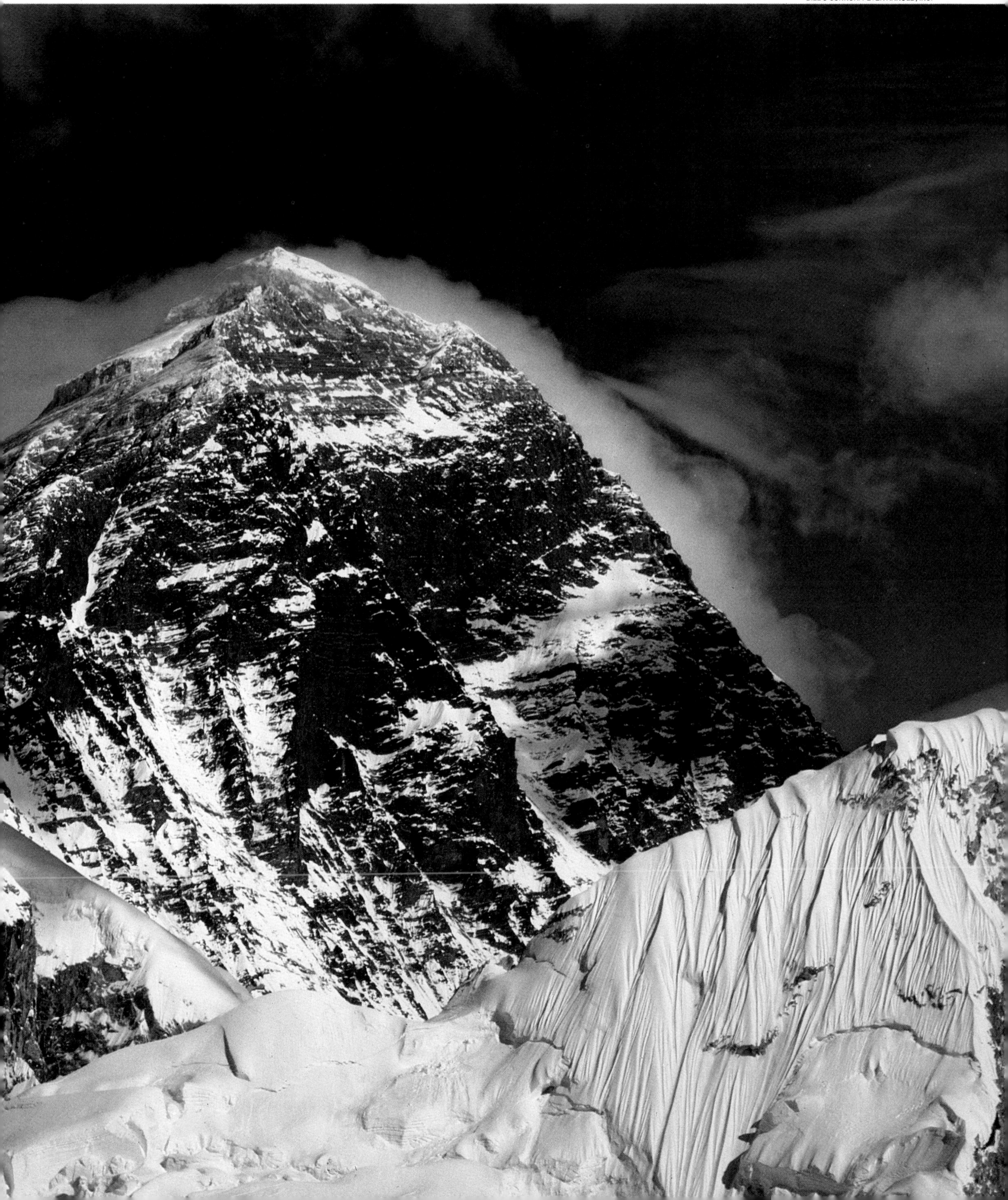

Buried Bones

Why did dinosaurs die out?

A life-size steel-and-concrete dinosaur rises above the treetops (above). This dinosaur, along with more than 20 others, sits in Prehistoric Gardens, a park in Port Orford, Oregon. People can model such creatures because scientists know much about what dinosaurs looked like. Scientists also know where dinosaurs lived. What they don't know is why the animals vanished 65 million years ago. That's a puzzle waiting to be solved.

The cartoon at right shows several possible answers to the puzzle, all combined in one imaginary scene. Over time, the land has slowly broken apart. Comets shower the sky. A dinosaur shivers as the earth chills, and two mammals huddle nearby. Mammals—animals that, when young, drink milk from their mother's bodies—were able to survive whatever killed the dinosaurs.

Many scientists think that the earth grew too cold for dinosaurs. The earth's crust is made of plates of rock that slowly move. Over millions of years, these movements have thrust up mountains and caused earthquakes. They have caused huge masses of land to break apart. Some scientists think such disturbances made the climate colder. They believe that even slightly colder winters and longer, drier summers might have been more than the dinosaurs could withstand.

Recently, some scientists have suggested that an asteroid—a chunk of rock and metal from space—or a shower of comets might have struck the earth about the time the dinosaurs died. A huge cloud of dust, they say, was thrown into the air. For a time, the dust blocked sunlight from earth, causing low temperatures and killing off plant life. This might have been the final blow to the dinosaurs.

Whatever happened, birds as well as mammals somehow survived. Their feathers or fur might have protected them from the low temperatures. Perhaps, one day, scientists will put all the pieces of the puzzle together.

How does a bone become a fossil?

For every bone that becomes a fossil, millions do not. It takes many thousands of years and very special conditions for a fossil to form.

Fossils are the remains of ancient life. At right, fossil bones poke out of the earth in the Badlands of South Dakota. Below, the body of a bison slowly decays. Although the bison's remains lie in the same part of South Dakota as the fossils, the bones probably will not last long. They will be destroyed by animals and by the weather.

To become fossils, bones must first be buried. Usually, that happens when an animal dies by a river, a stream, a lake, or an ocean. In such a place, water often washes sand, mud, and other fine-grained materials over the body. The soft tissue decays. The bones begin the slow process of fossilization.

Over thousands of years, minerals seep into the bones, changing them into fossils. In some kinds of fossil bones, the minerals fill tiny pores. As these minerals build up, the bones become heavier and stronger, but they keep their original shapes. Fossilization gradually continues until the bones have been completely replaced by minerals. Then we say the bones have become petrified—turned to stone.

TOM BEAN/DRK PHOTO

How can we tell the age of a fossil?

Scientists use many methods to find the age of fossils. Often they match up new discoveries with fossils whose ages are already known. The age of the rock surrounding a fossil may also provide a clue. The scientist at right is removing the rock surrounding the fossil bones of a small, three-toed horse. Like the bones above, this skeleton was found in the Badlands of South Dakota. Because scientists know the age of the rock layer containing the fossil horse, they estimate the fossil's age at 30 million years.

Sometimes scientists measure radioactivity to estimate age. All living things contain a radioactive form of carbon called carbon 14. After a plant or an animal dies, its carbon 14 gradually decays. By measuring the amount of carbon 14 remaining, scientists can estimate the age of the fossil—up to 45,000 years. After that, nearly all the carbon 14 has disappeared. For older fossils, scientists test surrounding rocks for various combinations of radioactive elements. As one radioactive element decays, it turns into another. Scientists measure the amounts of both. The more of the original element remaining, the younger the sample is. With such tests, scientists can date rock from 100,000 to billions of years old.

JIM BRANDENBURG/WEST LIGHT

Riches From the Earth

Why do cut diamonds sparkle?

Look at the pile of rough diamonds in the photograph above. You'll notice that the stones look shiny—but not brilliant. Then look at the huge Hope diamond and the smaller stones in the necklace at right. Those diamonds dazzle the eyes.

What's different about the diamonds in the two pictures? The rough diamonds have only been washed after mining. The stones in the necklace have been cut.

A cut diamond has many small, flat, angled surfaces called facets (FAS-uhts). The facets reflect the light hitting the stone and make the diamond sparkle. The top facets guide and bend the rays of light as they enter the diamond. The rays separate into colors. If the diamond has been cut properly, the lower facets act as mirrors, reflecting the light outward.

Centuries ago, before people learned to cut diamonds, Indian rulers wore the uncut stones. Finally, people discovered how to shape the gems. They found that only a diamond can cut another diamond. That's because diamonds are the hardest natural substance known on earth.

The Hope diamond, cut from an even larger stone, today is the largest blue diamond in the world. Mystery surrounds the Hope. According to legend, the Hope brings bad luck to its owners. Several owners of the diamond did meet with misfortune, but only the superstitious believe that the stone was the cause of the troubles. In 1958, the last individual owner of the gem donated it to the Smithsonian Institution, in Washington, D. C. There, it attracts millions of visitors each year. Some people go to see the Hope because of its beauty. Many more probably visit it because of its legend.

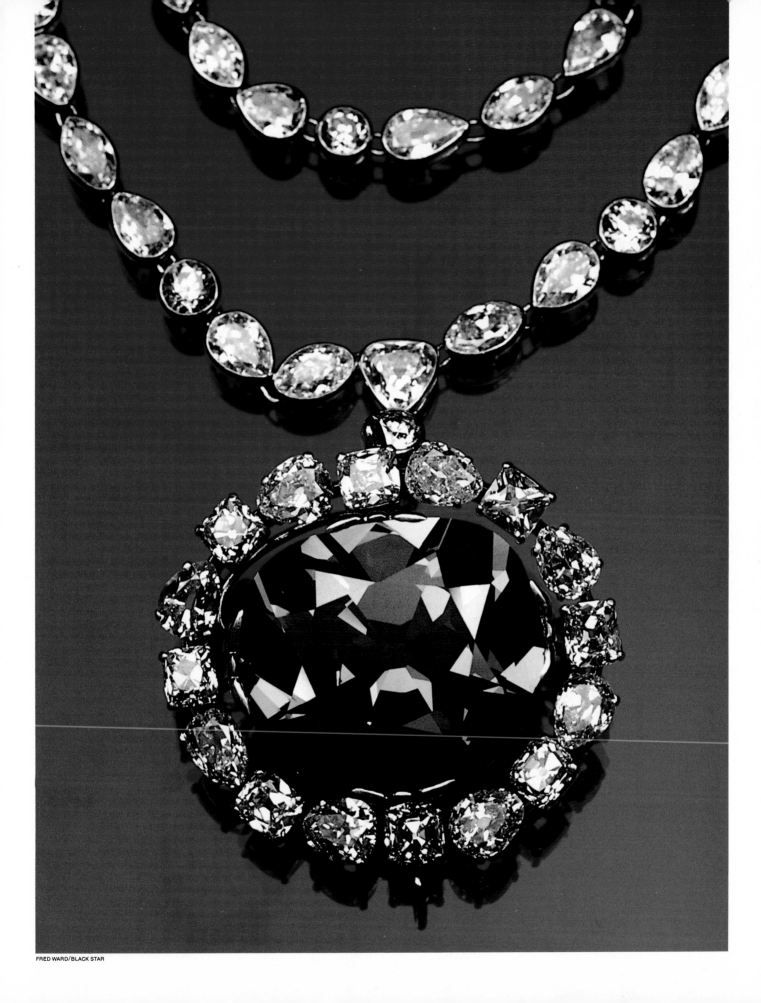

Why can you find gold in some streams?

They may be so small they can fit on a thumbnail, but shiny gold nuggets like the one below *do* lie on some stream bottoms. At left, a man pans a streambed in Alaska for nuggets and flakes.

The gold found in streambeds did not always lie there. Scientists think that gold formed long ago deep within the earth's crust. As gases and liquids rose to the surface, they carried dissolved gold upward. The gold-bearing gases and liquids oozed into spaces within rock. Gold crystals grew in the tiny openings, speckling the rock. In larger cracks and hollows, the gold formed deposits called veins.

Over time, the rock wore away. Water and wind broke off nuggets and flakes of gold. Rainwater washed them into streams.

Gold is nearly 20 times heavier than water and several times heavier than most kinds of rock. Although a rushing stream will carry with it flecks of gold, larger pieces will sink. They tend to become trapped in places where streams slow down.

Prospectors look for gold in pockets and holes along the inner curves of streambeds. Hollows around rocks or boulders also make promising panning places. The presence of gold in spots like these may hint that gold veins lie in nearby hills.

If you want to try your luck at panning for gold, visit an area where people have found the metal in the past. With a prospector's pan (left), pick up a load of water and bottom material from a stream. Swirl the contents around. Break up large clumps. Gold dust or nuggets will sink to the bottom. Tilt the pan so that the water flows out, carrying mud and sand with it. Remove the gravel. If you're lucky, you'll see some gold glittering in your pan.

Odd Rocks, Strange Sand

How can some rocks move across the desert?

Skid marks snake across the Racetrack, an ancient lake bed in California's Death Valley National Monument. The marks show that the rocks have moved. Scientists think rain or ice—and wind—caused the action. During some storms, rain makes the fine clay of the lake bed very slick. Winter freezes can have the same effect. Then, powerful winds blowing through the valley push the rocks over the slippery ground—sometimes hundreds of feet. The skidding rocks gouge shallow ruts in the mud. When the desert dries up again after a rain or a thaw, the mud—and the marks—become as hard as concrete.

How do sand dunes form?

Curving mounds of sand stretch toward the sky in California's Death Valley (below). Such mounds, called dunes, form when sand that is carried by wind meets an obstacle and piles up. Here, a trail of footprints marks the sand. Soon the wind will erase the prints.

Most dunes don't stay in the same place for long. The trillions of sand grains that form them are pushed by strong winds, whether in the desert or at the seashore. The shape of a dune depends on the amount of sand in it, and on the speed, steadiness, and direction of the wind that pushes it.

In places where winds blow from many directions, star-shaped dunes may form. When winds blow with equal force from two directions, an S-shaped dune may appear. Some dunes take on crescent shapes. Wind blowing from one direction picks up sand from one side of a mound and drops it on the other side. The middle grows thicker, and the ends grow narrower. A steady wind blows the ends ahead of the middle, forming a curve.

ART WOLFE/APERTURE PHOTOBANK

DAVID HISER/THE IMAGE BANK

What creates weird rock formations?

Some of the rocks in Canyonlands National Park, in Utah, have such unusual shapes that people have given them names. The formations above are known as the Molar and Angel Arch. Can you see why? At left, odd-looking towers called hoodoos rise out of the earth in Alberta, in Canada. Human sculptors didn't chisel these shapes; the forces of nature did.

Wind and water wear away rock in a process called weathering. The rock cracks, and water freezes in the cracks. As the freezing water expands, it widens the cracks. Some rock—like the sandstone in Canyonlands National Park—weathers easily, forming weird patterns. In a process called erosion, gravity pulls the crumbling rock to the ground. Wind and water from storms or streams carry away the pieces.

Hoodoos formed when surrounding land wore away, leaving rocky caps atop columns of rock and soil. The hoodoos got this odd shape because the hard rocks on top protected the softer columns from the effects of the weather.

How can a person get out of quicksand?

If you walked along the Little Colorado River, in Arizona, you might come upon the stretch of riverbank at right. If you stood on the ripply part of the sand, it would wiggle under your feet like gelatin. If you stepped farther out, to the sand covered with a slick of water, you might start to sink. You would have stepped into quicksand.

Quicksand occurs when water flowing through sand mixes with it to form a thick fluid. The quicksand may look solid and firm, but the grains are too far apart to support the weight of a person.

As a demonstration, the man below let one of his legs sink thigh-deep into a patch of quicksand along the Little Colorado. His other leg sank up to the knee. He then shifted his weight forward. Here, the weight of his body exerts pressure on his bent forward leg, and he drags the other leg slowly out of the mucky sand.

This procedure will usually allow a person to escape from quicksand. Sometimes it's necessary to repeat the steps. In this case, it took only a minute for the man to free his legs. Remember this way of escaping if you ever step into quicksand.

You can also get out of quicksand by stretching out on the surface, as if you were floating on your back in the water. Then you would slowly roll to firmer ground. Whichever method you use, the secret of escaping quicksand is to think quickly and move with purpose. A person who panics and thrashes about may only sink deeper into the sand.

MICHAEL COLLIER

MICHAEL COLLIER/STOCK, BOSTON

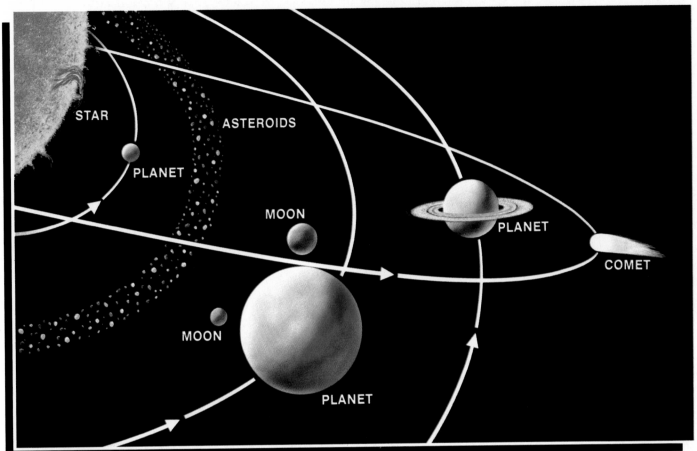

STAR
ASTEROIDS
PLANET
MOON
MOON
PLANET
PLANET
COMET

MARVIN J. FRYER

What makes up a solar system?

A solar system, like the imaginary one above, consists of a star and the objects that orbit it. The star is a spinning furnace that produces heat and light. The star's gravity controls the motions of the orbiting objects. They may be planets, moons, asteroids, or comets. A solar system may also include meteoroids, which are too small to show in this painting.

Most scientists believe that solar systems develop from vast clouds of dust, gas, and leftover matter from dead stars. Over hundreds of thousands of years, some of the cloud material contracts into a flattened, spinning disk. Particles spinning toward the center of the disk squeeze together. Their action causes the temperature to rise to millions of degrees. Finally, the center ignites, and a star is born. The star of our solar system is the sun.

In other parts of the disk, smaller lumps of cloud material collect and cool, forming planets and moons. Nine known planets wheel around our sun. Each stays in its own nearly circular orbit. Some bits

of material never come together to form planets or moons. Trillions of these bits—chunks of rock and metal called asteroids—tumble around the sun, most in a wide belt.

Comets are balls of ice, gas, and dust. Scientists believe that a huge cloud of comets orbits at a great distance from the sun. Occasionally, a passing star nudges a comet inward toward the sun into a looping orbit. Near the sun, some of the comet melts, releasing a tail of gases, and sometimes one of dust.

Whirling throughout our solar system are chunks of rock and metal called meteoroids. If a meteoroid passes through the atmosphere surrounding a planet, it heats up and begins to glow. Then it is known as a meteor. Some meteors hit the surface of planets and moons. They are then called meteorites.

Scientists are sure of the existence of only one solar system—our own. But they have photographs showing what may be others. Soon, using improved telescopes, they hope to have proof that others exist.

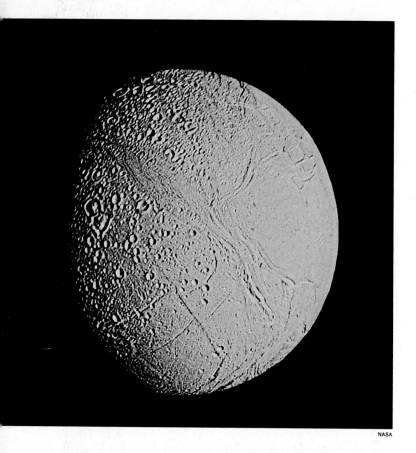

NASA

How do scientists predict when comets will appear?

Every year, about 12 comets streak past Earth on their way around the sun. Most are visible for a few days, weeks, or months. Then they vanish. Many return, though. A comet may reappear in less than four years . . . or in more than a million.

To predict just when, scientists observe the comet's location several times. They determine its speed and measure the angle of its path. From these observations, they calculate the size and shape of the comet's orbit. Finally, they predict how long the comet will take to complete its orbit. Some comets, called short-period comets, return in less than 200 years. One of these, Halley's comet, has reappeared about every 76 years for at least 2,200 years. Long-period comets, such as the Ikeya-Seki comet (below), appear much less frequently. This giant-tailed comet was discovered in 1965. Scientists predict that it will not return for 880 years or more.

Comets sometimes surprise scientists. Some comets change paths as a planet's gravity tugs at them. Others plunge into the sun, break apart, or fly off into space—never to return.

Do other planets have moons?

Many moons—more than 40 in all—orbit planets in our solar system. Only Mercury and Venus have no moons, or satellites. The other planets have one or more satellites, and those satellites have names. When we refer to them simply as moons, we are calling them by the name for our satellite—the moon.

Saturn has 17 moons—more than any other planet. One of its moons, Enceladus (above), reflects almost all the light that shines on it. That makes Enceladus the brightest body in the solar system besides the sun. Titan is the largest of Saturn's moons. It is larger than either of the planets Pluto or Mercury. Unlike most moons, Titan has an atmosphere. Thicker than Earth's atmosphere, it resembles a heavy layer of reddish brown smog. Scientists are not sure what lies under this layer, but they think an ocean of red liquids covers large parts of Titan.

Many of Jupiter's 16 known moons have icy surfaces. One, named Io, has erupting volcanoes that spout materials upward as high as 174 miles (280 km). The two moons of Mars are rocky. One, Deimos, has very little gravity. If you ran fast on Deimos and jumped, you would go into orbit.

Of the remaining planets, Uranus has five moons, and Neptune has two that we know of. Pluto has one, discovered in 1978. Who knows? There may be more moons yet to be found.

Is there life on other planets?

In our solar system, all the planets are too hot or too cold to support life—except Earth and Mars. Two unmanned Viking spacecraft traveled to Mars in 1976. Information collected by the craft showed no life. Most scientists now believe that, in our solar system, life exists only on Earth.

Planets in other solar systems, however, may have the right conditions for life. If life does exist, it is probably quite different from life on Earth. The imaginary planet in the cartoon below has a super-strong force of gravity. This force pulls gases toward the planet, creating a foggy atmosphere. The squatty creatures and low-growing plants have developed to suit the conditions. The cartoonist can only imagine what might exist in another solar system. No one knows. To try to communicate with other beings, scientists send radio messages into space. They have also sent picture messages and recordings aboard spacecraft. As yet, there have been no replies.

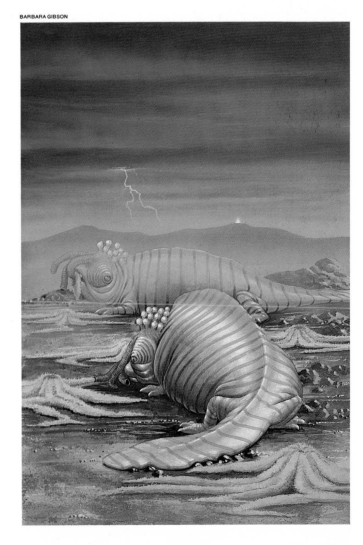

Why does Saturn have rings?

If you looked at Saturn through a telescope, you might count five or six rings circling the planet like a tilted halo. The photograph above, taken by the Voyager 2 spacecraft, shows even more rings. Closer photographs reveal thousands of rings—some wide, some narrow; some bright, some dark.

Billions of icy chunks form the rings that whirl around Saturn. Some of the chunks are the size of pebbles; others are as big as boulders.

We still do not know for sure how these rings formed. Many scientists now believe that the rings may be the remains of one or more old moons. Perhaps a moon orbiting too close to Saturn was pulled apart by the force of gravity. A comet may have struck a moon, shattering it and leaving the broken pieces to orbit the planet. Scientists have even found little moons in the rings.

The image you see here has been colored by a computer. The colors help scientists study the rings and other features of Saturn. Actually, Saturn and its rings are about the color of butterscotch.

At least two other planets in our solar system have rings. Uranus has nine narrow rings. All of them are as dark as coal dust. Jupiter has at least one thin, faint ring.

What is a nebula?

The word nebula (NEB-yuh-luh) comes from a Latin word meaning cloud. That's just what a nebula is—a huge cloud of gas and dust in space. Astronomers have discovered many different nebulae (NEB-yuh-lee). You can see only a few with your unaided eyes, but you can view hundreds through a telescope.

The gas in a nebula is mostly hydrogen, with some helium. Under certain conditions in space, the hydrogen and helium glow, creating a kind of bright nebula. In another kind of bright nebula, the glow comes from nearby stars. The dust reflects their light. Not all nebulae light up space, however. Sometimes the dust particles absorb light and create a dark nebula.

In both photographs on this page, you can see combinations of bright and dark nebulae. At left, the glowing gases of the North American Nebula paint the sky with color. This bright nebula gets its name from its shape, which resembles a map of North America. The outline stands out against a dark nebula—the area that looks somewhat like the Gulf of Mexico. The gleaming white dots are stars.

Below, a dark nebula that looks like a horse's head—the Horsehead Nebula—shows up against a rosy bright nebula. At the left in the photograph, stars buried in the dark nebula produce bright patches of white light.

JOHN A. BONNER, N.G.S. STAFF

What is a galaxy?

If you could see the Milky Way galaxy from a distance, it would probably look like the painting above. No one has ever seen all of this galaxy, however. That's because no one has traveled far enough from Earth to view it. Astronomers use information they have gathered to judge its size and appearance.

A galaxy is a huge grouping of stars, with nebulae, planets, dust, and gas. Our solar system is just a tiny part of the Milky Way galaxy. The arrow indicates the solar system's position. The Milky Way contains billions of stars and thousands of nebulae.

Astronomers group galaxies into four main types. Spiral galaxies, such as the Milky Way, appear to wind around and around outward from the center. Barred spirals look like spiral galaxies with a bar of stars through the center. Elliptical galaxies resemble watermelons in shape. Irregular galaxies have no particular shape.

Viewed from afar, the stars in a galaxy appear to be packed tightly together. Actually, vast distances separate even those stars closest to one another. Light travels at a speed of 186,282 miles a second (299,793 km/s). The Milky Way galaxy is so huge that light takes 100,000 years to travel across it.

As large as galaxies are, astronomers have discovered even larger groupings: groups of galaxies, called galaxy clusters, and groups of clusters, called superclusters. Powerful telescopes show groups of galaxies stretching endlessly into space. All together, these billions of galaxies make up the universe.

The Last Word

How do babies learn to talk?

The three-month-old babies in the picture below cannot yet talk. But can they ever vocalize! They make more sounds now than they may ever use in speaking—unless they learn many languages.

The ability to use language sets humans apart from all other creatures. Most scientists now believe that humans are born with a readiness to learn language. Researchers have found that babies respond to the human voice at birth. As babies listen to speakers around them, they learn to distinguish the sounds of speech. By three months, they make vowel sounds as they coo, chuckle, and squeal. Between their eighth and twelfth months, most babies combine vowels with consonants. That's when parents hear "ma-ma" and "da-da."

As babies grow, they listen to and imitate the words and voice tones of people around them. They begin to associate sounds with objects, actions, and ideas. By age five, most children speak well.

The early years, scientists say, are the best time to learn language. Not even college students can learn a language so quickly and perfectly as a child can.

JAY LURIE/WEST STOCK

Why do people speak so many different languages?

The children at right come from all parts of the globe. Each of them is bidding you a friendly farewell in a different language. The languages these boys and girls speak, however, make up only a small fraction of the world's 3,000-plus languages.

The expression each of these youngsters uses for good-bye represents sounds his or her people began using long ago to represent the thought "farewell." Throughout the world, groups have made up words and connected them to communicate with one another. In this way, many of the world's languages have developed.

As groups of people came together in war or in trade, they exchanged words and ideas. The languages of countries that sent off warriors often changed rapidly, as did those of the countries they battled. Each culture borrowed words and grammar from the other. Sometimes new languages arose. The pidgin English spoken on many South Sea islands, for example, is neither that of the English-speaking traders nor a native language. It's a blend of both.

How did the English language begin? Researchers think that English, most European languages, and Sanskrit, the language of ancient India, all point back to a single parent language. The original speakers split into many groups that eventually lost contact with one another. Their languages changed. In time, each variation became a new language altogether.

Many languages may be spoken within the borders of a single country. In certain places in the United States, you might hear people speaking Spanish, or Vietnamese, or Polish, or any number of other languages. If you traveled to the Soviet Union, you would hear many different national languages. To be sure you were understood in every corner of India, you'd have to speak more than 200 languages!

Mexico

Adiós
(ah-dee-OHS)
SPANISH

France

Au revoir
(oh reh-VWAHR)
FRENCH

Japan

Sayonara
(sah-YOH-nah-ruh)
JAPANESE

Kenya   (Official language: English)

Sére
(sair-REH)
MASAI

Good-bye !

Lebanon

Ma'a al-salāma
(mah-ahs-suh-LAH-muh)
ARABIC

Uganda   (Official language: English)

Kwaheri
(kwah-HAIR-ree)
SWAHILI

U.S.S.R.   (Official language: Russian)

Do pobachennya
(doh poh-BAH-chen-nya)
UKRAINIAN

Israel

Shalom
(shuh-LOHM)
HEBREW

India

Namaste
(nuh-muh-STAY)
HINDI

Federal Republic of Germany

Auf Wiedersehen
(owf VEE-dehr-zayn)
GERMAN

People's Republic of China

Zai-jian
(DZEYE-jee-yen)
CHINESE

Malaysia

Selamat Jalan
(slah-maht JAH-lahn)
MALAYSIAN

Index

ROBERTO VILLA/LEO DE WYS INC.

COVER: Does this gem look like a diamond to you? Actually, it's a cut glass imitation, according to experts. Imitation diamonds are shaped from glass, from quartz and other minerals, and from artificial stones. A real diamond has extraordinary brilliance, hardness, and fire—the ability to break light into colors. A fake—even a gem of a fake—won't measure up.

EDUCATIONAL CONSULTANTS
Glenn O. Blough, LL.D., Emeritus Professor of Education,
  University of Maryland, *Educational Consultant*
Nicholas J. Long, Ph.D., *Consulting Psychologist*
Violet A. Tibbetts, *Reading Consultant*

The Special Publications and School Services Division is grateful to the individuals and institutions named or quoted in the text and to those cited here for their generous assistance:

Bonnie V. Beaver, Texas A&M University; James D. Belville, National Oceanic and Atmospheric Administration/National Weather Service; Richard E. Berg, University of Maryland; Marilyn Berzin, M.D., Washington, D. C.; Barry C. Bishop, National Geographic Society; Merton Bowman, South Dakota School of Mines and Technology; Frank Busby, Busby Associates Inc.; Dewey Caron, University of Delaware; Valerie C. Chase, National Aquarium in Baltimore; Mark D. Clark, U. S. Forest Service; William A. Clemens, University of California at Berkeley; George J. Cohen, M.D., Children's Hospital National Medical Center/George Washington University; Larry R. Collins, National Zoological Park, Smithsonian Institution; Shirley Corriher, Atlanta, Georgia; Stuart Crump, *Personal Communications Magazine;* Raymon Davie, Monsey, New York; A. A. De Hertogh, North Carolina State University; Béla Demeter, National Zoological Park, Smithsonian Institution; Mark A. Dimmitt, Arizona-Sonora Desert Museum; Michael D. Duncan, Naval Research Laboratory; Sylvia A. Earle, California Academy of Sciences; Thomas C. Emmel, University of Florida; Beverly Evans, Corning Glass Works; Miklos Faust, U.S.D.A., Agricultural Research Service; A. Budd Fenton, D.V.M., Alexandria, Virginia; George Fenton, Fenton Art Glass Company; Frank H. Forrester, McLean, Virginia; Michael W. Fox, The Humane Society of the United States; Joseph Golden, National Oceanic and Atmospheric Administration/National Weather Service; Larrie Greenberg, M.D., Children's Hospital National Medical Center; John T. Hack, U. S. Geological Survey; Dick Hallion, History Office, Edwards Air Force Base; Robert S. Harrington, U. S. Naval Observatory; Richard L. Harris, Padre Island National Seashore, National Park Service; Jessica A. Harrison, University of Arizona; Henry Heikkinen, University of Maryland; Bill Hershberger, University of Washington; Thomas A. Jenssen, Virginia Polytechnic Institute and State University; Terry R. Kerby, National Oceanic and Atmospheric Administration/Hawaii Undersea Research Laboratory, University of Hawaii; Charles A. Knight, National Center for Atmospheric Research; Loren E. Lane, Mount Rainier National Park; John Langbein, U. S. Geological Survey; Howard Lawler, Arizona-Sonora Desert Museum; Russell E. Lee, National Air and Space Museum, Smithsonian Institution; Herbert W. Levi, Museum of Comparative Zoology, Harvard University; Bob Maida, Manassas, Virginia; Miles L. Mellette, Potomac Electric Power Company; Larry E. Morse, The Nature Conservancy; Eugene Morton, National Zoological Park, Smithsonian Institution; Jennifer Moseley, National Geographic Society; Junie Nathani, Intelsat; Thomas T. Nigra, M.D., The Washington Hospital Center; Virgil Olson, Death Valley National Monument; Donald Petzold, University of Maryland; Jon Radtke, Death Valley National Monument; David Raup, University of Chicago; Mark P. Richards, U.S.D.A., Agricultural Research Service; John Risdon, Identification Division, Federal Bureau of Investigation; Patrick Rivalan, Intelsat; Solomon Sara, S.J., Georgetown University; Henry W. Setzer, Curator of Mammals, Emeritus, Smithsonian Institution; Sally Shuler, Fairfax County (Virginia) Public Schools, Lacey Instructional Center; Henry G. Siegrist, Jr., University of Maryland; Steven E. Smith, Arlington Public Schools Planetarium; Norman Steele, U.S.D.A., Agricultural Research Service; Peter B. Stifel, University of Maryland; Mark K. Stowe, Museum of Comparative Zoology, Harvard University; Clint Vincent, Jr., U. S. Parachute Association; Robert D. Warmbrodt, University of Maryland and U.S.D.A., Agricultural Research Service; John S. White, Smithsonian Institution; Brian Wood, Bell Atlantic Mobile Systems.

Library of Congress CIP Data
Main entry under title:
  Why in the world?
  (Books for world explorers)
  Includes index.
  Summary: Questions and answers on a wide range of subjects, including geophysical sciences, physiology, natural history, physics, and technology.
    1. Science — Miscellanea — Juvenile literature.   2. Technology — Miscellanea — Juvenile literature. [1. Science — Miscellanea.   2. Technology — Miscellanea.   3. Questions and answers]   I. National Geographic Society (U.S.)   II. Series.
Q163.W493 1985   500   85-18862
ISBN 0-87044-573-1 (regular edition)
ISBN 0-87044-578-2 (library edition)

WHY IN THE WORLD?

PUBLISHED BY
THE NATIONAL GEOGRAPHIC SOCIETY
WASHINGTON, D. C.

Gilbert M. Grosvenor, *President*
Melvin M. Payne, *Chairman of the Board*
Owen R. Anderson, *Executive Vice President*
Robert L. Breeden, *Vice President,
Publications and Educational Media*

PREPARED BY THE SPECIAL PUBLICATIONS
AND SCHOOL SERVICES DIVISION

Donald J. Crump, *Director*
Philip B. Silcott, *Associate Director*
William L. Allen, *Assistant Director*

BOOKS FOR WORLD EXPLORERS
Pat Robbins, *Editor*
Ralph Gray, *Editor Emeritus*
Margaret McKelway, *Associate Editor*
Ursula Perrin Vosseler, *Staff Art Director*

STAFF FOR *WHY IN THE WORLD?*
Jane R. McGoldrick, *Managing Editor*
David P. Johnson, *Picture Editor*
Drayton Hawkins, *Art Director*
Sharon L. Barry, Jacqueline Geschickter, Theresa K. McFadden, Susan McGrath, Anne E. Mulherkar, Catherine O'Neill, Susan Tejada, *Writers*
Debra A. Antonini, Laura L. Austin, Bonnie Piper, *Researchers*
Ross Bankson, *Contributing Editor*
M. Barbara Brownell, Martha Reichard George, Sheila M. Green, Catherine D. Hughes, Jennifer Kirkpatrick, Gloria LaFay, Suzanne Nave Patrick, Eleanor Shannahan, *Contributing Researchers*
Susan Crosman, *Research Assistant*
Joan Hurst, *Editorial Assistant*
Bernadette L. Grigonis, *Illustrations Assistant*

GAME: Patricia N. Holland, *Special Projects Editor*

ENGRAVING, PRINTING, AND PRODUCT MANUFACTUR
Robert W. Messer, *Manager;* David V. Showers, George V. White, *Production Managers;* Gregory Storer, *Production Project Manager;* Mark R. Dunlevy, George J. Zeller, Jr., *Assistant Production Managers;* Timothy H. Ewing, *Production Assistant*; Kevin P. Heubusch, *Production Staff Assistant*

STAFF ASSISTANTS: Dianne T. Craven, Carol R. Curtis, Lori Elizabeth Davie, Mary Elizabeth Davis, Ann Di Fiore, Rosamund Garner, Virginia W. Hannasch, Nancy J. Harvey, Linda Johnson, Katherine R. Leitch, Ann E. Newman, Cleo Petroff, Stuart E. Pfitzinger, Pamela Black Townsend, Virginia A. Williams

MARKET RESEARCH: Mark W. Brown, Joseph S. Fowler, Carrla L. Holmes, Meg M. Kieffer, Barbara Steinwurtzel, Marsha Sussman, Judy Turnbull

INDEX: Teresa P. Barry

Composition for WHY IN THE WORLD? by National Geographic's Photographic Services, Carl M. Shrader, Director; Lawrence F. Ludwig, Assistant Director. Printed and bound by Holladay-Tyler Printing Corp., Rockville, Md. Color separations by NEC, Inc., Nashville, Tenn.